*Thanks to spouses, PMI,
people of each continent for lessons!*

PERFECT PHRASES™

for

PROJECT MANAGEMENT

Hundreds of Ready-to-Use Phrases for Delivering Results on Time and Under Budget

Helen S. Cooke, PMP
Karen Tate, PMP

New York   Chicago   San Francisco   Lisbon   London   Madrid   Mexico City
Milan   New Delhi   San Juan   Seoul   Singapore   Sydney   Toronto

Contents

Preface

Project management has been around for thousands of years, but it is only in the past few decades that it has been structured as a professional management practice, with processes and methods that work time after time. If you are reading this book, you are most likely involved in a project or are about to be. Project management is a field of work populated by individuals who have chosen this particular practice of management as their profession. Some project management professionals are specifically project managers. Others can be program managers, scheduling specialists, or experts in some specific functional area unique to projects. The Project Management Institute promotes common definitions and standards so that people who work in project management can work together across occupational and geographic boundaries. In the publication of the *Project Management Body of Knowledge (PMBOK Guide®)*—one of its key standards—projects and project management are defined. A project is a temporary endeavor undertaken to create a unique product, service, or result, and project management is the application of knowledge, skills, tools, and techniques to project activities to meet the project requirements. Projects are carried out by people, and special roles and rules apply when managing teams and getting results within specified constraints. Traditional managers can enlist the help of superiors in resolving problems or allow time for things to work themselves out. Project managers need to identify solutions and get results quickly within the team. While some projects are not large or complex enough to require a certified professional in every role, others are. The people who manage projects of significant importance and complexity, such as the launch of a space shuttle or a new energy processing facility, often have certified project management professionals in every key role on the project. But even smaller or less complex projects benefit by good project management. Many of the good practices across projects are presented throughout this book.

Since a project is a temporary endeavor, it has a clear beginning and a clear end. Projects are launched to create a unique product, service, or result (referred to as deliverables). It can mean doing something for the first time, and doing so in such a way as to minimize risk and maximize intended outcomes, reorganizing something in a way different from what it was before, integrating complex changes into an existing environment, improving things to operate in a new way, or creating new products or services.

If we could get desired results doing things as we have always done them—using normal operations processes, for instance—we would not need to create a project. We would simply get it done. But for many kinds of projects no normal operations processes exist. The projects are formed because key results and products and services are vital, yet they simply cannot be produced doing things the way we have always done them. We need a new way to do it, perhaps a different mix of people or a different combination of processes or a completely new product or service. Project management offers ways to manage the risks and unknowns that come with creating something new. The new product or service is created by the project manager and team using project management. Then it is handed over to operations, who assume responsibility for its use, maintenance, and improvement.

Project management is a broad management discipline crossing all occupations and industries using recognized tools and techniques based on global standards. Projects are managed in a similar way around the world. When an organization manages work using familiar day-to-day business processes, these routine processes have been refined by repetition as people perform their daily tasks. Periodically the processes are improved by experienced workers. Most experienced workers are familiar with them and can quickly form work teams to get things done. With projects, this luxury is not available to the team. Very often, new processes and ways of doing things have to be defined anew.

Because each project is unique, the project management processes become the team's new structure for performing work. The organization that typically has departments, job descriptions, and supervisory reporting channels also has accepted measures of work effectiveness and product quality. On a project, these same needs exist, but the methods, roles, and rules on a project are not the same as the ones used when performing routine work. It is the responsibility of the project manager and team to create the work structure for the project and define acceptance criteria and requirements. Projects are generally "one-off."

The project team members will need to know how to work together, with role descriptions, reporting channels, policies, and quality measures for their work. They may be more narrow and simpler, but they still are necessary to structure work and guide team decisions during the project period. Many organizations that rely on projects to do their work and keep their products and services competitive in the marketplace will have project management processes, roles, and management support systems in place that are built just for running projects. Others do not.

Whether your organization is experienced at running projects or new to the process, whether it has a project management infrastructure or not, this book can provide value. The phrases in this book will help you state the needed ideas the team members must address or, by your words and communications, shape the expectations and involvement of managers, customers, and users of the project's eventual product or service.

As you read through this book, take the parts that are most helpful to you and pass them along to the project managers and team leaders who work with you. Adapt and shape the suggestions in this book to the context of your work or the cultural requirements of your work setting to deliver the results you intend, with quality, timeliness, and efficiency.

Introduction

Phrasebooks are not about presenting the reader with new management models or concepts. They are about translating concepts into words for success in specific situations. *Perfect Phrases for Project Management* is one such book. However, just as the authors need a solid grounding in project management concepts, standards, and practices to offer sample phrases that can be used to guide managers and team leaders to project progress, similarly the reader needs a grounding in project management concepts and practices to lead others to success. Your personality, work environment, coworkers, and even cultural setting will shape how you manage. We invite you to see this book as a starter kit with which you can build your own perfect phrases for project management.

What Is Project Management?

If you are a manager launching new projects or a project manager leading a project team toward successful delivery of results, you need quick access to the working concepts that can skillfully guide subordinates, team members, customers, and operations workers toward implementing projects and delivering business value from projects. That means you need not only the right phrases for the task at hand but also the right concepts about project management to deliver success. First, some definitions. These were provided by *The Guide to the Project Management Body of Knowledge*, or *PMBOK Guide*, Fourth Edition, published by the Project Management Institute, a global professional association in Newtown Square, Pennsylvania, that has clarified and defined project management and the work of project management professionals since 1969:

- "A project is a temporary endeavor undertaken to create a unique product, service, or result (deliverables)."

- "Project Management is the application of knowledge, skills, tools, and techniques to project activities to meet the project requirements."

- "A program is a group of related projects managed in a coordinated way to obtain benefits and control not available from managing them individually. Programs may include elements of related work outside of the discrete projects in the program."

- "Deliverable(s) are any unique and verifiable product, result, or capability to perform a service that must be produced to complete a process, phase, or project (final or interim)."

Launching a project often involves attempts to meet a defined business need or resolve a problem using routine methods; a decision that a project is called for to get it done; and a process of early definition and decisions about the type of project and its end deliverable or result, referred to as project initiation.

When the decisions that result from these discussions are formalized, usually in a charter or authorization document, adequate information is available to create a high-level plan for the project, describe the necessary characteristics or benefits of the end product, make broad estimates of "how much and when," and propose an approach. This high-level plan is not definitive enough to commit resources or propose delivery dates, but the general requirements, constraints and limitations are sufficient to block out a detailed plan that can be refined by those doing the work. Often the critical success factors for both the project and its end deliverable are specified and the scope of the work has clear boundaries of what the team will or will not be expected to do, the plan is approved and the work commences once the project has moved into execution.

The natural risks that come with doing something for the first time are mitigated by the application of project management. Trained project management professionals apply their knowledge, skills, methods, tools, and techniques in iterative clarification of the project's tasks, and once the plan is approved and the team appointed, the work is carried out under systematic monitoring and control until the end product is finished and turned over to those who will put it to use. At closeout, the work is done, the agreement is closed, and the resources and records are filed for future reference. The project is over.

The same process occurs on large and small projects across disciplines and industries. They may be conducted internally or contracted out, often depending on their sensitivity, specialized nature, or importance. The methods and formalities may differ and the technical approach and standards vary across industries. But projects are projects, many of them important, complex endeavors, and they need project management to be successful. Many new or popular approaches, beneath the surface, may be recycled old approaches to projects, simply with a different name. Projects are pretty much the same across industries and cultures. Each project has a single project manager; people assigned to support the work and track the results; and processes to initiate, plan, execute, monitor, control, and close the endeavor. But *management* is the key word. Managing something that is being created for the first time involves unknowns: risks, challenges, and issues that have the potential to mature into real problems. Fortunately, project management is designed to address them using knowledge, skill, processes, tools, and methods that turn potentially unpredictable outcomes into predictable and systematic progress toward the project's objectives.

Using project management processes and the project management body of knowledge also allows the project manager and team to define those objectives using common terms and address changes to them as the project progresses. The product, the characteristics of what is delivered, even the name may change. But the professional who manages a project has a whole toolbox of tried-and-true methods to move a project toward its successful conclusion. These "perfect phrases" capture the essence of those methods, although the actual work may be more technical than the discussion. The challenges are often unseen by the customer or sponsor of the project. What makes a good project manager shine is the ability to tap the whole arsenal of knowledge, tools, techniques, and methods to deliver the desired end product.

Many sponsors of projects do not want or need to know all that goes on within the project. The project manager and team are given not only the responsibility for delivering results but also the authority to make the decisions needed to get there. Freedom to adapt, change, and lead the team are crucial to making the decisions and taking the actions that enable success.

If you can't get it done using the organization's standard operations, it probably is a project. When that decision has been made, then the team proceeds to determine the best approach based on the project objectives. Many of the decisions made early in the process of creating a project help set the stage for project success. Picking the right leader, the right tools, and the right team members to get desired outcomes are also critical. Finally, the team needs support from senior management to navigate organizational threats or barriers to success.

The right leadership, the right decisions, the right support, the right methods and tools set the stage for success.

These "perfect phrases" can help get you there.

PART

PROJECT MANAGEMENT

Project management is the application of knowledge, skills, tools, and techniques to project activities to meet the project requirements. Since a project is a temporary endeavor, it has a clear beginning and a clear end. Projects are launched to create a unique product, service, or result.

CHAPTER  1

Project Management Concepts

Often you hear the words *project management* in conjunction with the phrase "on time and on budget." Achieving results on time and within the allocated budget is a major requirement of any project. To manage a major project in that way means a lot of people did a lot of things right. It is never "magic," however. It is the result of managerial wisdom, discipline, and skill. Here are some of the fundamentals of project management that many people never see. It is important that the project manager and team:

- *Work with management to define project success.* If you do not have a clear definition of project success, you will not be able to develop critical success factors for management, the user, and the customer. You will have a hard time deciding whether the product or outcome of the project is "done." And if you do not have those critical success factors before you begin to plan or staff the project, you will find it extremely difficult to redesign the outcome to meet the satisfaction of the stakeholders.

- *Describe the final deliverable product before the start of planning.* It is a good general rule that if you cannot describe the final deliverable (i.e., product, service, or result) of a project in substantial detail, you will have great difficulty estimating the cost to produce it or the time frame in which you can deliver.

- *Identify the deliverables, tasks, and activities needed to create the final deliverable.* If you cannot describe the work in adequate detail to estimate how much time it will take and assess the resources needed, it is too early to put work tasks into a project scheduling and tracking system.

- *Involve the customer or user of the project—or a surrogate— in developing the design specifications and functionality of the product.* Involve the project stakeholders in the project. If the people who will apply or use what the project creates are not involved in defining success, the project can be technically successful and still fail in delivering the benefits to the sponsor and customer, or be declared a failure by the greater community. If the stakeholders are not included, they can slow or even stop progress.

- *Set a target date to finish the work and close the project.* If you have no project date for delivery, you will not have a basis for reevaluating the process to refine it. Rely on careful and realistic estimates to create your target dates and budgeted costs. If you do not have reasonably accurate estimates against which to track the project, you will be going through a bureaucratic exercise to report on its status, because the plan will not be reliable enough to use its data for decision purposes or the decisions made on the basis of those status reports will be unfounded.

- *Get the customer to sign off on the final product before you end the project.* If you cannot obtain acceptance of the product, service, or outcome of the project from the operations group or customer when you complete the work, you are not "done" and will not be able to close out the project and send team members back to their regular job (or the next project).

- *Record suggestions for improvement and pass them on.* If you have no mechanism for capturing "lessons learned" on the project and feeding them into the systems and processes of the next project, the next project may not be any more successful than this project was. Even if you are fortunate enough to get the same talent on the next team, often the same mistakes are repeated.

How much formal project management you need will vary based on how long or complex or challenging the project turns out to be. And such decisions are ideally made before beginning the project work. But fortunately, project management is designed to handle just such ambiguities. In the chapters to follow you will find phrases to help communicate some of the key project management concepts to your sponsors, team members' management, customers, and operations personnel who rely on you to lead them to a successful project conclusion.

Project Phases/Processes Summary

Project initiation—A process to authorize a new project that helps ensure that the project manager, project team, project customer, and project sponsor understand the goals and constraints of the project in the same way and align it with its work/resource environment.

Project planning—A process used to develop the project management plan that helps the team to document and formally gain approval for the resources required to carry out the project and to achieve the project objectives within project constraints; the plan, once approved, provides a baseline for tracking and correcting variances during execution.

Project execution—A process used to perform the work described in the project plan, along with various project management functions such as monitoring and controlling, to ensure the project objectives are met. Completing the process of project execution means completing the work defined in the project management plan prior to project closure.

Project monitoring and controlling—A process used to identify, define, and correct variances from the intended process for performing project work during the entire life of the project so that the project's objectives are achieved. Project monitoring and controlling help to ensure adherence to the project management plan as well as maintaining an environment for success for the project team. Cyclical meetings and reports that are part of this management process provide information on project status and trends to ensure that the plan is being followed and kept up to date, and making controlled changes that are needed so the project objectives can be met.

Project closeout—A process used to finalize the activities of the project, meet legal and administrative obligations, document results and lessons learned, distribute any remaining resources, and formally close the project. Completing the process of project closeout ensures that all project work is complete and that the project has met its objectives.

Roles and Responsibilities

There are common roles and responsibilities for the launching of a new project. The most common are those of individuals who fund, lead, staff, and expect the benefits from projects.

Project sponsor—The person accountable to meet the project's overall objectives and to provide project oversight. May also be called the project champion. Role: Management representative who initiates or approves the project and is accountable for the success of the project. A sponsor often provides the project's funding.

Project manager/leader—The person assigned by the performing organization to achieve the project objectives. A project manager makes management decisions. Role: Leads the project team and is accountable to meet the project objectives.

Project team member—The person or people assigned to the project to create specific deliverables, or to perform a defined technical or management function. Role: Participates on the project team and is accountable for their deliverables.

Project customer—The person or group that accepts the final deliverables. Role: Represents (or is) the user and is accountable to provide requirements for the deliverables and accepts the final deliverable (product, service, or result).

At times the project customer and project sponsor may be the same person, especially for internal projects within a single organization. Funding for projects may come from the sponsor or customer or both. In some cases, the customer is in a separate organization altogether or is a member of the general public. Occasionally the project team can be brought in from outside the sponsoring organization. On a large or complex project there may be many distinct roles on both the project management team and the technical team, including scheduling specialist, risk specialist, procurement specialist, and others. The specialized roles on the development or technical team will vary by the type of project and the industry, as, for example, an oil field geologist, a field anthropologist, an avionics technology expert, a software developer, or a nuclear plant safety engineer. Since the occupations and specialties of people on project teams vary so greatly, this book addresses only the project management side of the project.

General Start Questions

Since projects are different from so-called normal operations, they must be managed differently. Unlike the workers who work together regularly in "normal operations," the team that is assembled to carry out the project may be drawn from different work groups and even different organizations, and their terminology, definitions and work methods may vary. Therefore, some of the first questions that need to be answered are those that frame your entire verbal approach to others. Projects are somewhat unpredictable, and looking at snapshots of project activity at any single point in time may or may not represent how well the project is going. Letting people know that projects bring with them a certain number of risks and unknowns can help them become less nervous if things do not look as smooth or as predictable as a similar activity would look under daily operations.

Because of the potential challenges projects bring, people do not usually undertake them lightly. Projects are begun because people need their results and believe that the resources, time, and diligence necessary to create their products and services are worth the investment. But their need for the project's results does not necessarily mean they are confident that the project manager and team are capable of delivering those results.

When projects succeed, people focus on the benefits of the final product or service—what project management teams refer to as their final deliverable. Very little of the discussion after a successful project has closed focuses on the quality of project management that led to success. But when projects fail, or their outcomes are not fully realized, there is plenty of press coverage. The same might be said of firefighters or police or public safety officers. When they do their jobs well, the results are taken for granted. When something goes wrong, it gets headlines! But the public is more familiar with those roles, and they have gained public respect over the years.

When people are familiar with project management, the project manager and team still can earn the right to be trusted.

Gaining trust is more challenging if the sponsor and customer of the project are not familiar with the team's leaders and have little information with which to gauge the project's likelihood of success. Once a trust relationship had been established, however, then the project manager can confidently ask for their commitment to support the project team and allocate the needed resources to finish the project. They may be asked to provide support and backing even when success is still uncertain. So it is important when just getting started to ask a few questions to see what is needed to establish a trust relationship.

Perfect Phrases to Start a Project

- Do the sponsors and customers of the project know me and trust me to deliver results?

- If the sponsors and customers do not know us well, how do we earn their trust?

- The confidence of others will grow as we continue to demonstrate our competence, knowledge, and integrity in this effort. Until then, we can provide documentation of our track record to validate their confidence in us.

- First, let us learn who the different people are who need to trust us, and figure out what they will consider evidence that they should trust us.

- How should we be interacting with the key players? What behavior do they expect of us?

- How should we be presenting information to them? What are they accustomed to seeing?

What information is most vital to them? Does this differ from prior projects we have done?

Who is most likely to benefit from our project's success, and who stands to lose if we don't succeed?

What has been done to confirm the validity of the project? Any feasibility studies?

Was there a cost-benefit analysis done on this project to show it is worth the investment of time and money?

What examples can we give them from our experience to show that we will likely succeed?

Who is the best person to put forward as a competent manager, technical expert, or advisor?

What provides the best example of our capabilities, knowledge, skill, and ability to get results?

PART

PROJECT INITIATION

roject initiation is the process used to define and authorize a new project. It is the first step in creating a project, and it places the identified need or opportunity into proper context with the executive portfolio and organization's strategic initiatives. If approved, the documentation from project initiation ensures that the project manager, project team, project customer, and project sponsor understand the goals and constraints of the project in the same way. After the initiation process is complete, the business case, problem or issue definition, and project objectives are condensed into a charter suitable for approval by management. The charter captures adequate information to plan the project at a high level and begin to build an environment for project success. The project charter—whether by that name or another, such as proposal or authorization form for funding—is what documents and formally authorizes the existence of a project as the basis for project planning. It provides the project manager and team with high-level project objectives and articulates the project constraints. Once created, the charter is usually approved by the project sponsor or customer. Depending on the organization, the project charter can be prepared by one of the following—the project initiator, the project sponsor, or the project manager—with input from the others. Documenting initial understandings and assumptions at the beginning of a project is important because project planning is iterative, and its elements and conditions can change.

Part of what is considered in creating a new project is how the new project relates to the executive portfolio of projects, the strategic initiatives already in place, and the identified need or opportunity that the project is created to address. Alternative ways of meeting the need are often considered before beginning a new project. Sometimes other options have been tried unsuccessfully. When the appropriate executives and subject matter experts review the alternatives and commit the organization to proceed with planning a new project, there are a number of key questions that need to be answered. These answers are captured and included in the project charter, which serves the project team as a reference document that forms the basis for planning. Once the charter is approved, the key managers and subject matter experts can begin to block out the project, with appropriate information on requirements for the final deliverable, approved resources, and any limitations and constraints placed on the project by management.

CHAPTER 2

Perfect Phrases to Identify the Need for a Project

U sually projects are created because the important outcome or desired result could not be achieved by other means. But it is not unusual for people to make a project out of something because it gets full attention, resources, and team commitment as a project that it might not otherwise get. Yet, climbing on the project management bandwagon can be counterproductive if it inserts different management knowledge, methods, and techniques into what is already working well.

Perfect Phrases to Determine If This Is Really a Project

- Are you sure we really need to make a project out of this? Could it be done through operations?
- What has already been tried, and how did it turn out?

- Why can't we get this done the way we do everything else around here?

- A project has a defined start and a defined finish: how long a period do we expect this project to run?

- Who is a likely candidate to manage the project? Could it just as easily be given to a business or technical analyst as part of their normal workload?

Perfect Phrases to Clarify Why a Project Is Needed

- There are many reasons to put a project in place: increase revenue, cut costs, or respond to regulatory requirements. Why is this one necessary?

- Is this a high-, medium-, or low-priority project compared to other things that are going on?

- This is going to take a good amount of resources; what makes us think we are going to get them?

- Who considers this effort particularly important? Why?

- What if we decided not to do it?

- Is there more than one group or division that is going to benefit by what we do?

Perfect Phrases to Distinguish Project Management from Operations

- We will be managing this work as a project instead of "business as usual," and using project management processes.

- Who is experienced in this kind of work, in managing projects like this?

- Is this going to be a major effort, requiring management attention over months or years, or can it be completed in a few weeks?

- If it is not a big effort, does it really need to be managed as a project? Can it just be a job assignment to someone in the department?

- Who in the organization can ensure this can be done, and done effectively?

- This work should have the right person to manage it, with the authority to make it happen.

- Who "owns" the project?

- Has a project manager been involved in preparing the proposal? Who is the project manager? If there isn't a project manager assigned to it yet, who is championing the effort?

- Has anyone been considered to head it up? Who are the potential candidates?

- Have any technical experts been identified that would be needed for success?

Perfect Phrases to Clarify the Purpose and Value of the Project

- We need to tie this to the strategic plan: what strategic goal does it support?

Projects are how we implement the strategic plan. What strategy would this project advance? Who is responsible for implementing that strategy at the executive level?

Where will the product (or service) be placed under our operations groups when it is done? How will it fit in with what they are doing now?

Who will "own" the deliverable that this project produces? Do we have information on what will be happening with what is created and how it is expected to be used?

What precisely will the project team be delivering at the end of the project?

I know it is much too early to be giving it a name, but if you were to pick a nickname, what would you call it?

Who will be the owner of the final product when the project is over?

What is the project team's responsibility for putting it in place or making it work as it should?

Are there any barriers we need to know about that could make it difficult?

Are there any other projects going on or planned that could affect this project?

● What are the benefits we expect from this project? Can they be delivered by this project alone, or will they be a combined effort of other projects as well?

Perfect Phrases to Identify the Project's Sponsor or Champion

Will this project be important enough to place this in the hierarchy where one manager can make all the key decisions across groups?

Who cares that this project succeeds?

Who has a history of backing successful projects?

● How is the project funded? Who has the spending authority to back this project?

Who is the end customer? Who understands the user?

Has an executive already been assigned as this project's sponsor? Is that person positioned to take ownership of the product or ensure the resulting service from this project? Will it be handed off to another executive to deliver the benefits?

Is our sponsor an effective communicator to ensure continued support from every group involved in our project as well as the executive team?

If our sponsor is not high enough in the organization to resolve all the problems we might encounter across group lines, how can we find that person or get that support?

Who has the financial power and political influence to defend the project if it runs into organizational barriers? Are they behind this effort? Who can get their support?

- Who can ask the right questions to help develop the project boundaries and constraints?
- What do we need to do to make that sponsorship official?

Perfect Phrases to Identify Managerial Constraints and Assumptions

- How do you think this work can be achieved? How do you envision this working out over time?
- How long could it take, and is that too long?
- What does top management expect? What will the end user—the customer—expect? Are these the same? What constraints do we have? Will the executive team approve the assignment of key people to this project?
- What about resources? We can't predict what it will take this early in the planning process, but how much money or effort is too much?
- Is there anything that we absolutely have to do or can't do? Is it acceptable to increase the number of people on the payroll or change the computer system? Is there any area we must not interfere with or change?

Perfect Phrases to Define the Project's Success Measures

Sometimes a project is considered successful if the project team simply delivers what was defined as a product or service for the customer. Acceptance criteria for the end product of the project should be objective, not subjective. Objective criteria can be observed, counted, or collected in "evidence." Subjective terms such as *acceptable*, *compatible*, or *satisfactory* rely on the judgment of a single person or group, and those judgments can change over the course of a project. The project team will need SMART objectives to determine if the end result of the project has met its criteria or not so they will know if they are done. SMART objectives also guide the planning process. Here are some helpful phrases to clarify these points for use by the team as they develop the list of tasks they must perform to create the final product, service, or result.

- Can we state the project goals clearly and describe how we will verify they are met?

- Will those goals, once met, make a measurable, meaningful contribution to the organization? How will we know the project made a real difference?

- How much of that contribution can be attributed to the project's deliverable(s)? How much might be the result of other factors, such as new partnerships or access to new markets? Has anyone quantified the value of those other factors?

- SMART refers to *specific, measureable, achievable, realistic, time-bound*. Are the goals SMART? (See page 54.)

- Are those goals likely to be met when the project is complete, or long afterward?

- Management usually has a clear idea of what makes a project successful, but sometimes these ideas are not well defined for the team. Success measures should be numerical or in accordance with a standard or objective definition. One way to capture success measures is to define subjective terms in writing for later reference. (For instance, what is an "economical" car, 25 miles per gallon? 35–40?) Another way is to ask, "Can we articulate the project objectives in concrete terms?"

● The project objectives are typically what the organization hopes to achieve after the project's execution.

● Project objectives vary, but some success measures might be expressed as:

   ❖ Scope/Deliverable + Acceptance Criteria
   ❖ Time/Schedule + Deadline
   ❖ Cost/Cost Estimate + Cost Limit
   ❖ Effort/Effort Estimate + Effort Limit

CHAPTER 3

Creating the Project Charter

Regardless of the name placed on the initiating documents, every project needs a formal document outlining the project's goals, objectives, sponsor, general scope, assumptions, major constraints, critical success factors, and leadership. Common terms for this document are charter, proposal, authorization, or approval. Projects need a formal document to capture the key assumptions and constraints under which the project manager and team will operate because things change as projects progress, and everyone needs a place to review the project parameters. They are formally approved after planning, but if the parameters change, or assumptions prove to be incorrect, the project manager and team need formal changes in these agreements to guide their work and their decisions.

Perfect Phrases for Discussing Project Goals and Benefits

● We now have a business leader who will sponsor our project and support our success.

Since we have a sponsor and project goals, do we need to develop a formal business case?

What are the sponsor's goals for the project? How do they align with overall strategy?

What are the organizational benefits that will accrue after the project deliverable is complete and in place? Is this project part of a larger program? We need to know that.

What are the benefits to the users of the end product? Are the project's customers the users, and are they known, or can we make any assumptions about the users and user benefits?

Do we have a standard format for recording the project's scope, stakeholders, reporting, requirements, limits, and constraints as we develop them?

Who is approving the final charter (or proposal) and how do we formalize that approval?

We need to make the project sponsor role clear and official to the organization.

In developing a charter, we need to define the general scope for the project, any project assurances that management will need to see documented, and what type of a team the project will need to carry out the objectives.

Perfect Phrases for Discussing Project Scope

What is the business problem or opportunity of this project? How this problem/opportunity is defined will affect the final deliverables as well as customer expectations.

● When the project is finished, what are the expected operational results? The expected impact on the project customer's organization or business can deliver desired results or fall short. If we want to know we have succeeded, we should express the desired impact of the project either as an aspirational or a numerical goal.

Who is the person who will approve the final deliverables for the project? Will it be the project customer? [The customer is often the person or group that accepts the final deliverable of the project and converts it to use.]

What are the project decision criteria for this project? Which is most important—faster, better, or cheaper? Ranking of scope, schedule, and cost criteria by their relative importance helps when making decisions that require trade-offs.

● What are the high-level, early customer requirements? There will usually be specific features or functions of the final deliverable that are important to realizing the benefits.

● What are the final deliverables of the project? [The word *deliverable* is an easy way to describe the product, service, process, or result that will be given to the project customer.]

Sometimes it is difficult or premature to put a name on the final deliverable until the project—and how it will meet the business need—is better defined.

● What are the final deliverables acceptance criteria?

Project objective for scope is the criteria the project customer will use to determine if all the important things have been completed and the final deliverable is acceptable.

- Are there any organizational deliverables expected from carrying out the project? The organization may gain a new capability (product, service, process, result). [Often in exchange for the commitment of time and resources, the project is expected to produce organizational benefits in addition to the final deliverable.]

- An additional product, service, or process to be created for the organization (not the customer) may be a firm expectation. If so, what are the acceptance criteria?

- What major stakeholders (groups, departments, other projects) does the project need to consider? [These would be groups other than the customer and team that will be affected by the project.]

Perfect Phrases for Discussing Project Quality

- Project teams are seldom given carte blanche and infinite resources. What are the constraints under which this project will operate?

- What is the desired level of project risk (risk limit)? [The risk limit is the amount of risk the organization is willing to accept on the project in exchange for the benefits it will gain.]

- Are there any required reviews and approvals (sign-offs, tollgates)? If so, which deliverables will be the ones where review and approval are necessary?

- Are there any checkpoints for assuring the quality of the final deliverable requested by the sponsor? [These are usually early enough in development to make corrections or improve conformity with the customer's requirements.]

● Are there any status reports or other reports required? If there will be periodic reports (requested reports), what are they? When should the team produce them? [The project team will be asked to keep certain documentation, typically what is needed by management to monitor the project as it progresses.]

Perfect Phrases for Discussing Project Resources

● What about team assignments? Who is assigned to the project team? The early plan can list job roles or titles, but we will need names or groups assigned to the project team for every task in the plan.

● Are there any deadlines? Deadlines are not discretionary; they are dates we must meet (project objective for schedule). [Dates that must be met, including completion of the final deliverable, are often critical to achieving the benefits of the new product or service, and not meeting those dates could make the project a failure.]

● Is there an effort limit for the project? [The organization committing the resources often will have defined a maximum amount of effort permitted to be spent on the project.]

● Is there a cost limit? What is the maximum amount of money we can spend? [The project objective for cost is the maximum amount of money authorized for the project.]

- Exceeding the effort and cost objectives is often tied to the return on investment (ROI), whether financial or simply the relative importance of this project within the organization's larger priorities. Do we know the ROI defined by management?

- Are there any organizational constraints for this project? Things we are required to do or not allowed to do that have been spelled out by management? These constraints—other than deadlines, effort, or cost—are limits that the project must live by.

Perfect Phrases for Developing the Charter

- Let's develop the document that describes what is expected, and do it in simple terms.

- Whether it is called a charter or a proposal does not matter so much as what goes into the document and how it is used.

- The charter should contain the answers to the main questions about the project.

- First, what are the business reasons for the project—simply stated?

- What is the team expected to produce as a result of the project? What is the end product?

- How much risk is management willing to accept from the project? Is there a risk limit?

- What deliverables does management want to review or approve? Just the key deliverables?

- What status reports does management want to see? Many status items are just for the team.

- Who should lead the project teams (team leaders)? Who will be on the project team stated in the charter?

- What are the objectives of the project? How will management know we have met them? What are our early projections of final and interim deadlines? Can we state it in a range? We will not know how much there is to do or how long it will take until we do more detailed planning.

- What are our preliminary effort estimates? Can we state that in a range, also? Minimum means we can't do it for less, without changing the requirements. Maximum? That probably falls within the resource limits of what management will approve for the project.

- What are our preliminary cost estimates? Do we include human resources or just capital expenditures? What is the minimum we think is needed in actual cash outlay?

- Are there any other constraints on the project?

- What are the priorities for the project if we have to make hard choices among alternatives? What does the customer want? More features, faster delivery, better quality, cheaper production?

- If we have to choose among taking longer, costing more, or maintaining quality and scope, what does management want us to put first?

- Can someone write this up so we have a permanent record available to the team?

PART III

PROJECT PLANNING

P roject planning is the process used to develop the project plan, including managerial and technical tasks required to complete the project. It is used to document and formally approve the resources required to achieve the project objectives within project constraints, and to provide a baseline during execution for monitoring project progress and controlling variations and risks.

The project management plan is prepared by the project manager and the project team and approved by the project sponsor and/or project customer. The high-level plan created from managerial objectives and constraints, with detail added by the team, becomes a formal, approved document detailing how the project work will be executed, monitored, and controlled as well as how the deliverable of the project will be created. The project management plan includes more than just the tasks that describe the work of the project; it also contains information on the project's environment, risks, integrated schedules, and interim deliverables and costs. Strategies for communications, quality, and team development are also reflected in periodic activities within the work plan. Inputs to project planning include the project charter and the business case, the objectives, and the user's needs. Completing the plan and getting sign-off authorizes the project team to proceed within the approved resources. The outputs of the planning process include the management tasks, detailed activities, deliverables' acceptance criteria, refined estimates, and a staffing plan, as well as the post-project review criteria to be applied at closure.

CHAPTER 4

Perfect Phrases to Set the Stage for Project Planning

Planning is not always easy, and many people are willing to charge ahead with a project with just an undocumented cursory plan. But can you imagine going on a long vacation without thinking through what you were going to do, where you needed to be, how you would get there, and what you needed to take with you before you left home? It is less efficient and riskier to vacation unprepared, and the same principle applies to project management.

Because projects are different from the normal work routine, they need to be planned. As the leader of the planning process, you need to clarify the objectives of the project and what will be considered a successful outcome, just as you would need to identify the objectives of your vacation and how you would determine if it had been a success when it was done. But how much planning do you really need? Some say you plan as much as you need to so you can sleep at night. This means you have enough information to feel confident about the project. You do

39

not need so much detail that it insults your workers' individual capability, generates more information than is needed to perform work, or requires oppressive control to carry it out. Remember, if it is in the plan and generates a deliverable (that is, an interim product or service), it will need to be tracked. Tracking is not free. It consumes time and resources, and too much can distract team members from their work. A plan should provide efficient guidance.

How much detail you need to manage the team's progress and how much detail upper management needs are often not the same. Some managers who supervise the project manager or fund the project just want to know about changes that affect the project's agreed-on outcomes or commitments. How the team gets it done is delegated—it becomes the responsibility of the team and its project manager.

Perfect Phrases to Clarify Why Planning Is Necessary

- Do we have a clear understanding of what this project is expected to produce?

- Once we have clear objectives for the project, we will need to plan how to get there so we can provide some direction for the team members to do their work.

- Where do we stand now on these objectives? Is that our starting point for the team?

- Regardless of what we call it, what will the end deliverable have to be able to deliver?

- There may be many ways to approach creating the end product; are any "out of bounds"?

- If we can block out an acceptable range of costs and dates, the team can add the detail.

- We need to create a project plan to reflect what we can deliver.

- Project planning is what we call the process used to develop the project management plan.

- The purpose of the planning process is to document and formally approve the resources required to achieve the project objectives, and get management support to spend them.

- Of course, we will need to stay within any project constraints set for us by management as well.

- Tracking our actual work against the plan allows us to see if we are staying within those limits and constraints (the project baseline).

Perfect Phrases to Estimate a Range of Dates and Costs for Delivery

It is tempting to estimate a delivery date and overall project cost when first deciding to do a project. But until the work is blocked out and reviewed by the people who know what it takes to do that work, these estimates are more like "guesstimates" than viable projections. No public announcements or promises should be released until the plan has been reviewed and adjusted by the experts, and projections should be expressed in terms of ranges (10 to 12 months, 2 to 3 years). Nevertheless, estimates are necessary in order to decide whether the project is worth doing, and to budget for it.

The project management plan, once it is complete, will have to be approved by the project sponsor and/or project customer, but it needs to be prepared by the project manager and the project team because they are the ones who know how much time and resources the work will require.

A formal, approved plan becomes the team's road map. It not only details how the project will be executed, monitored, and controlled so the project stays within its budget and meets deadlines, but it also usually contains information on risk, integrated schedules, interim deliverables and expenditures. These are perfect phrases you can use as you define these elements.

- We have many of the high-level descriptions of what the project is supposed to produce and when management expects it will be done.

- Are there any existing limits on what we can do or how that affects when we think we will be done?

- Can we assume we have all the resources in the world to do this, or are there resource limits placed on us by the sponsor or customer?

- It is hard to estimate how much work this will take, but does anyone have an estimate of the time and effort it would take if everything turned out just perfect or went just perfectly and we had the ideal team to do it?

- What would be the latest date we could finish before it was just no longer worth doing?

How many years or months will have passed before that latest possible date?

Can we express it in elapsed years/months before we overlay the work on the calendar?

If we have our earliest date we can deliver, and the latest management will accept, can we assume something in between would be a reasonable range for completing the project?

Are there any schedule constraints—holidays or mandatory training programs planned—that the team will be required to attend during that period?

Perfect Phrases to Discuss the Real Risks Associated with Projects

You seldom get a good reception when you say "this might not work out," but there are real risks associated with doing something for the first time.

Projects often have time limits and therefore need to be carefully managed to prevent overruns.

Resources are scarce, and time and talent allocated for doing the project work can be eaten up resolving unexpected problems.

Often the best way to prevent unexpected problems is to identify as many of them as you can, and plan how you will either prevent them altogether or deal with them one-by-one if they should materialize.

Some problems will surface as general issues or push back during early discussions, and these can be recorded for later reference.

Some problems are outside the control of the team, and some are even outside the control of top management. Those are the problems you will find yourself dealing with as a team.

Expend your resources addressing the unexpected problems, not the "predictable" problems you could have planned for.

We can identify potential problems by telling stories or by giving examples from projects that have happened in the past. If those problems might occur on this project, we should record them and manage them using risk management.

Let's make a list of risks and issues, and delegate them to a member of the team to track and manage.

Perfect Phrases to Begin Discussions About Project Risk

There was a time when I/we tried to _____ (give an example of a project situation) and this is what happened when we did.... How could we prevent this from happening again?

Could we put that into concrete terms? How much money did it consume (cost, lose, waste)?

Have things changed since the last time we tried a project like this?

How bad would it be if we started this and then for some reason could not finish?

What might prevent this project from succeeding that you know of—or might even suspect?

I heard of a project in the news (example) that cost two to three times what they estimated, but the project still finished well and people were happy with the result. What if this project ran over budget?

We have done projects similar to this in the past. Did they end up costing more than we planned? Was the project still worth doing?

How bad would it be if we just decided to cancel this one? Is there a risk to not doing it at all?

What if we did it well and generated a good useful result, but just delivered it late?

If the team was faced with a trade-off, what is most important: on time, on budget, or quality?

Who would be the biggest losers if things did not work out as planned?

Would anyone be glad to see it scuttled? What can we do to win them over?

Perfect Phrases to Define What Type of Project Is Needed: Scope

Some projects are created just to plan or design something, such as a community redevelopment initiative or a product prototype. Other projects are expected to define it, research it, plan it, design it, build it, test it, install it, and make sure it actually works before the project is considered done. What kind of a project is this one?

● Sometimes extensive thought, studies, and research have been carried out to decide something is worth doing. Has anyone worked through the concepts around this project? How do we know whether it is worth doing, and how can we tell if it succeeds?

● For some projects, those who want to create something new have already outlined the functional or technical specifications of what they need; the project just implements what has already been decided. Has anyone gone so far as to specify what we need to develop?

● On other projects, just an idea or need has been generated, executive management delegates the rest to a project sponsor or champion, and the team is expected to develop the project from scratch. If we are not able to find the research or justification already prepared for us, we may have one of these projects on our hands.

❖ Some project types, such as complex construction projects, are put in place one project after another—the end result of one project is the starting point for another, and entirely different knowledge and skill is required for each. These could rarely be just one project, even if the organization had the entire range of capability. At other times, the problem or product is so complex that it can only progress for a short period before it becomes too complex to plan. Will we be doing a lot of small mini-projects in a series to develop the end product? Could the deliverable be a plan for creating a completely new project?

❖ If the scope of what the project is responsible for is not black and white, when in doubt, ask. The answers may spark disagreement among those who want the project but whose expectations differ. Clarifying the scope of the project early helps avoid controversy later. After all, you cannot plan what you have not defined. We may as well define it up front.

❖ The project sponsor should be able to help us define what the project is expected to do, and probably also help define what it will not do (that is, define the scope boundaries of the project). We can find out from him what the project is going to look like.

Perfect Phrases for Clarifying Scope Boundaries with Management

● Are we just looking to design this, or do we actually need to build and install it?

● Who takes care of integrating it with the other type of work going on in this area?

● Are there other projects that will be dependent on the outcome of this one?

● Are there any parts of this effort that depend on something that has not yet been set up?

● If the time frame and cost are hard to meet with this broad definition, can we split it up?

● Could more than one group do parts of it simultaneously and integrate it later downstream?

● Do we have all the skills needed to do this, or will we need to subcontract any part of it?

● Can we document the project scope for future reference: our goals, objectives, strategic alignment, management assumptions, and constraints?

● Where will we store key documents like this for team reference? Where does the organization keep project documents for future reference?

● Have there been any projects similar to this one in the past that we could use for reference? There may be task plans or risk descriptions that could help us out.

Identify and Track Issues That Might Arise

Some say that issues are not problems to be resolved, but they can develop into problems. Therefore, identifying issues is a wise preventive practice. Issues begin to arise in the earliest stages of project initiation and continue through closeout. Creating an issues list and making it available to the team allows each team member or stakeholder to articulate an identified issue when it raises its ugly head, whether or not it will become a real problem later on. Some issues will surface in the earliest discussions about the project, and others will not be apparent until a lot of work has already been done. If the time in the project when that issue was expected has come and gone, and nothing surfaced, simply remove the issue from the list and add new ones from work stages yet to come!

Perfect Phrases to Discuss Issues

- Issues are not problems; they are ways for us to realize things we do not know and need to look into. But although they are not problems, they can develop into problems if they are not addressed. We should keep a list, and systematically address issues until they are resolved.

- Some issues just disappear as work progresses. If so, they can be dropped from the list.

- To identify issues we may have missed, are there any areas of the project that are not yet firm?

- Are there any areas that are seemingly fixed in place but that we are not confident we know enough about? Lack of knowledge can evolve into an issue.

- Perhaps it is too early to tack down all the unknowns. When we get into some detail in the plan I am sure we will find questions we are not prepared to answer. When those questions arise, we can track them as issues until we find an answer.

- The project manager starts the issue list early on, during project initiation. Who will manage it down the road?

- Let's keep the issue list in a common file so the team has access to it 24/7.

- For every issue, we need to identify someone qualified to address it.

- If someone identifies an issue, she may see something we haven't seen yet. Record it.

- People who push back may have an issue underlying their reluctance. Who is resisting? Can someone talk with them to find out what is behind it, and add it to the list?

- Not every issue becomes a problem. If the time passes and nothing occurred, drop it from the list. Add new ones for work we have not gotten to yet.

- If we have a hundred issues, there are probably a "top ten" and a "top three" at any one time that have the most potential to become problems. Focus attention on the important ones first.

- Every issue is important to someone, just not to everyone. Do not ignore issues just because they seem unimportant to you. Our work is interdependent. There can be a ripple effect.

CHAPTER 5

Perfect Phrases to Define the Scope and the Boundaries of the Project

The project's sponsor can help define what will be done in the project and what is considered out of bounds. But high-level boundaries are like a fence around the project. They are not specific enough to make work assignments or guide what will be developed and when. When initiating a project, you may have to ask a lot of questions to get specific about what you are expected to deliver. Only then can you put a plan in place to manage the work. It is best if you involve the team in defining the work of the project, because it builds morale and commitment. If the team is involved in creating the elements of the plan, they understand the importance of their work in carrying out a successful team effort.

A good place to start Project Plan Development is to develop a brief and complete description of the deliverables that will be produced by the project. Earlier we identified the outer boundaries for the project—what is outside the scope of work. A scope description covers what will be produced inside the project itself—what the team will actually create. The deliverables will be produced for the customer and, where appropriate, for the organization. Therefore, they must satisfy the acceptance criteria if the project is to be a success. By asking the team to develop the description of the project's deliverables and the deliverables' acceptance criteria, each team member will have a better sense of how the work he or she does contributes to the success of the entire project. By involving them in scope boundaries discussions, they are less likely to initiate work that is "out of scope" and squander valuable project resources.

The purpose of a scope description is to detail the deliverables that will be produced for the customer. A single description of the deliverables is important to make sure that everyone understands what the project is intended to accomplish and to make sure the final deliverable will satisfy the customer's needs and requirements. To help the team to know when they are done with their work and the project can close, they need to describe how the project's final deliverable will satisfy the customer's acceptance criteria.

Perfect Phrases to Define Acceptance Criteria

- We want our customer to be satisfied with the result of our project. Whatever acceptance criteria we define early in the project for our final deliverable will also be put to use when we near completion. We need to make sure our acceptance criteria for the deliverable is "SMART" so it is easy to see if the product or deliverable is ready to be turned over to the customer.

● SMART is an acronym made up of the first letter of each characteristic we should look for when we describe the criteria for judging the adequacy of our end product when the project is complete:

❖ S stands for *specific*. Acceptance criteria should be specific: that means it can be understood only one way and is free of ambiguities and unverifiable terms. Acceptance criteria should also be stated positively, and preferably in numerical form. There is less ambiguity if the criteria are stated in a form that elicits a "yes/no" response. Finally, acceptance criteria can be stated as "being in accordance with" an established, understood, and recognized definition, procedure, or standard.

❖ M stands for *measurable*. Measurable items can be verified.

❖ A stands for *achievable*. Things that are achievable can be done within project constraints.

❖ R stands for *realistic*. Things that are realistic make sense. They are believable and well grounded. If it is realistic, it is also appropriate for meeting the requirement that the customer or sponsor has specified for accepting the project deliverable.

❖ T stands for *time-bound*. Items that are time-bound can be identified and counted (how many) at some specified point in the project or simply noted as being present (yes/no format).

Perfect Phrases for Discussing Interim Deliverables

● As we plan the project, interim deliverables is a phrase we can use to describe the deliverables that are produced along the way to completing the final deliverable. The customer may or may not see them, but they are important to the team in managing our work progress.

● It is important to determine—in sequence—what deliverables will be produced before the final deliverable is completed because progress in creating interim deliverables can be useful in tracking progress against the final deadline.

● When the larger deliverables are broken down into interim deliverables, it is easier to assign accountability to individuals on the team map and to identify the interdependencies among them. It also helps us know who is affected by our work.

● To track schedule progress, our project task list first breaks down the final deliverable into manageable and tangible steps. As steps are completed, each of you can see how you are progressing in your work over time. We will each report progress in status reports so we can see how the whole team is progressing (we sometimes call it "tracking status").

● To define key accomplishments of the project, we establish a milestones schedule.

- Milestones can be used to monitor progress at a high level during execution. Milestones are often helpful in reporting to management.

- If a deliverable is defined as 100 percent complete, it can be checked off (yes/no) and the team can move on to the next development effort.

Perfect Phrases to Define Interim Deliverables

As a team, we will need a deliverables list before we can create a schedule. How do you develop a deliverables list? You can work in teams to develop one.

When you already know what to do, ask, "What is the first deliverable you will produce?"

- What are all the deliverables you will need?

What is the last, or final, deliverable?

What is the sequence for creating these deliverables? Put them in order.

If you can, use an existing template or refer to a similar project to check your list. It can help to make sure you are not leaving anything out.

When you aren't sure how to begin, work backward! Start from the final deliverable and ask yourself, "What do we need to have before we can create this deliverable?"

When things are really vague, brainstorm. Ask for ideas of deliverables from members of the team and list them.

- Team members can suggest things "off the top of their head" without criticizing anyone's ideas until there is a good list of items to evaluate. Then sort them. (Criticism inhibits creative ideas!)

- Is it an unfamiliar or complex project? Brainstorm the interim deliverables as a group.

- If you need to brainstorm, here is a method for brainstorming in a group setting: Place chart paper at the front of the room and hand out sticky notes to participants. Then ask everyone to write down his or her ideas on a sticky note, read them aloud, and slap the note onto the chart paper until it is full of notes. Put the sticky notes in sequence order on a table top or wall, starting from those that occur early in the schedule to those that occur at later points.

- Define the acceptance criteria for only those interim deliverables that could have a significant impact on the quality of the final deliverable.

Perfect Phrases to Define Where the Project Will Begin and End

- A project boundaries analysis can help to define what is inside and what is outside the responsibility of the project.

- Defining the project boundaries helps the team to communicate exactly what the project will do. We need to be able to clearly define the responsibilities of the project. We also need to manage people's expectations of what we will or will not be doing on the project so we get fewer unreasonable requests.

● Can we state clearly where the project begins and ends?

● Is there overlap or conflicts with other projects? If so, what are the project interfaces? How will we resolve any fuzzy areas if boundaries are not clear?

● We may need to coordinate our efforts with other groups or projects.

Perfect Phrases to Identify the Items That Are and Are Not a Part of the Project Scope

● Do we know all the stakeholders or groups that will significantly affect the project?

● Do we know all the groups that will be affected by the project?

● Who are the people, processes, and projects that will provide inputs to our project?

● Who will receive outputs (deliverables) from our project?

● Are there any other initiatives that will affect or be affected by our project?

● Let's list other projects that may have scope overlaps with our project—or that could impact or be impacted by the work of our project.

● How will we identify and monitor issues that are caused by these other projects?

● Who on the project will monitor these for us? Maybe we should include someone from those other projects on our project team.

● Let's include a task to do this analysis in the project plan.

Perfect Phrases for Creating the Project Work Breakdown Structure (WBS)

The work breakdown structure, most often referred to as the WBS, is a list of the work to be executed by the project team according to the deliverables they will be producing. The team will accomplish the project objectives and create the required deliverables as they move through the project life cycle.

Each descending level of the WBS represents an increasingly detailed definition of the project work, and a representative on the project team will be responsible for completion of that work stream's final deliverable. (See Appendix A for example.)

To create the WBS, the project team leaders use the Work Breakdown Structure Dictionary, which describes each component in the WBS with a brief definition of the scope or statement of work, defined deliverables, a list of associated activities, and a list of milestones. Other information may include the responsible organization, start and end dates, resources required, an estimate of cost, charge number, contract information, quality requirements, and technical references to facilitate performance of the work.

The work breakdown structure, once created, shows a deliverable-oriented hierarchical decomposition of the work to be executed by the project team to accomplish the project objectives and create the required deliverables. It organizes and defines the total scope of the project and allows management visibility into project progress and performance.

Once the WBS is finalized, the project team is able to establish control accounts for each of the work packages and place a unique identifier on each of them from a code of accounts. These identifiers structure the costs, schedule, and resource information in a way that can be not only summarized for the subproject but also used to measure performance of the project as a whole.

To establish project controls, these control accounts are placed at selected management points in the WBS. Each control account may include one or more work packages, but each of the work packages must be associated with only one control account. Then, when management wants to evaluate the project's performance using earned-value methods, the information can be integrated—scope, cost, and schedule—into one single point of the project.

Not every project or every organization uses earned value to measure project performance, but for those that do, the work breakdown structure is an important management feature.

Perfect Phrases for Discussing the Work Breakdown Structure (WBS)

● What is the best way to divide up the work of the project to track progress?

● A WBS organizes and defines the total scope of the project in one structured package. It divides the entire project into manageable chunks (subprojects) with a common code.

● If we use this format, we can create a Tree Diagram for quick visual reference.

Once we define subprojects, a project team member can be assigned accountability for each one.

With assigned accountability for completing each of the major segments of project work, we can quickly track how well we are progressing toward completion.

We will also need to define how we will finalize the final deliverable of each subproject. Each subproject leader needs a way to determine when he or she is "done."

Perfect Phrases for Organizing the Team on Subprojects

To begin the process of coordinating the work efforts we can empower team members to both plan and monitor their piece of the project.

If we empower the teams, the core team and the project manager will be able to stay focused on the main parts of the project and leave the details to the subprojects.

The team member assigned to be accountable for each subproject will be the subproject leader.

The subproject leader is accountable for the deliverables of the subproject. This doesn't mean that the subproject leader creates all of the deliverables himself or herself; it only means that he or she ensures the deliverables are created.

We should create a graphic representation (organization chart) of the project and the breakdown of the final deliverable. We can show who leads each group in the chart.

Let's create the list of subprojects based on the way the project work will be done.

We can organize subprojects based on functional areas/departments, geographical region, business unit, customer, or product lines. We could also organize them based on calendar or industries. What works best for this project?

Even though more than one subproject may use an interim deliverable, only one subproject will produce it. Include it on the branch of the subproject tree that is accountable to produce it.

We don't want to leave anything out. We need to agree on the final deliverables that each subproject will produce, and make sure that each interim deliverable of the project is included in a subproject.

Let's not forget to include a subproject for "Project Management." This subproject captures project-management deliverables (charter, project plan, status reports, closeout report) and often the final deliverable, since project management is responsible for the success of the entire project.

If we review the WBS with the team, we can delete any duplicate deliverables, add any missing deliverables, and do a final review with the team (and others as appropriate) before finalizing the WBS.

Planning: Project Scope—*Summary*

Activity	What to Do	Questions
Scope Description	Develop a complete description of the final deliverables that will be produced by the project. Create a Deliverables Table.	What are the customer requirements? What are the features and functions of the final deliverable? What are the criteria for accepting the final deliverable? Is it SMART? Is it clearly defined?
Interim Deliverables	Identify the interim deliverables for each final and organizational deliverable.	What deliverables will be produced in order to create the final deliverable? What interim deliverables require internal acceptance criteria?
Project Boundaries	Determine what is included and is not included in the scope of the project.	What items are and are not included in the project? What departments, areas, and stakeholders should be considered? What other projects overlap/ interface with the project?
Work Breakdown Structure (WBS)	Break down the project into subprojects (work units) and define the subproject deliverables.	How can the project be broken down into subprojects? Who will lead each subproject? What will each subproject produce (final and interim deliverables)? Who is accountable for each deliverable?

Perfect Phrases for Creating the Task List

- The scope of work includes all the tasks the project team will have to complete to deliver the final deliverable (give name) at the end of the project. Both project management tasks and technical tasks are in the plan. Together, they comprise the scope of work on our project.

- Since the plan is approved by management, everything in the task list is within the approved scope of the project.

- If it is not on the task list, it is probably not part of our scope of work—although there can be things we overlooked.

- Don't add tasks to the plan without approval: we can't afford "scope creep." Ask first!

Perfect Phrases to Clarify What Major Tasks the Project Team Will Be Expected to Do

- The project charter identifies the products or deliverables we are expected to produce.

- Based on what we have agreed to produce by the end of the project, and the approach we may decide to take to complete the final product(s), there will be a sequence of major tasks we will have to do first. Those tasks are in the high-level plan and eventually will be developed in greater detail in the detailed plan.

- Each of you on the team is being asked to review the task list and ensure we have all the tasks listed that you know you will have to complete to perform your work. If a task is missing, add it.

- Every task requires time, effort, and resources, so as we add detail to the plan, the overall project schedule and budget become more defined.

- Once we have a well-defined task plan for the project, and a complete work breakdown structure (WBS), then we can begin to discuss realistic delivery dates and a range of budget resources it will take to get there.

- Based on the tasks we need to accomplish, and projected personnel and costs associated with those tasks, we can ask management for a budget to work with.

- Even though a high-level budget may not be accurate, it is good enough for us to enter into an agreement with management. They deliver the budget and resources; we deliver the products and benefits.

Perfect Phrases to Clarify What Tasks the Project Team Will Not Do on the Project

- We have been given a high-level budget to carry out what we have agreed to do. It does not cover tasks or activities that were not part of that approved plan and budget.

- The scope boundary is like a fence around the project: If it is inside the fence, it is our responsibility. If it is outside the fence, we don't have to do it.

- If people ask you to do something that is not in our plan, tell them you have to ask first. If the argument is compelling, we can always ask for more money if we have to.

- It's going to have to be pretty important for me to go ask for more money, but we can.

Perfect Phrases to Deal with Fuzzy Areas or Interfaces with Other Projects

- We should identify any areas that may change during the project that could affect our work.

- The possibility of change has the effect of stopping the momentum of the team.

- We try to anticipate problems before they occur, and fuzzy areas can contain problems. Is anyone aware of things that could get in our way as the project moves forward?

- Are there any systems, programs, or company relationships due to change in the near future?

- When things are changing, the environment we are working in at any point in time can be different from what it was a week ago. Things we take for granted and rely on may not be there.

- Does anyone know of any obsolete systems or programs scheduled for removal?

- Are there any departments we are working with that are undergoing market changes?

Are there any stakeholders working with our project who could let us know if things change?

Is an operations group, like accounting or finance, experiencing regulatory change that could affect our project? Who would know? Is there a quick way to find out?

Can we talk with them and get an agreement from them to alert us if our project might be affected?

Who are the best people to do it—both on their end and on our end?

● Can we appoint a member of the project team to serve as a liaison with that area?

Are there any other departments or stakeholder groups we should be paying attention to?

● Is anyone aware of other projects going on in the areas we are working in, or that can affect us?

What is the best way to coordinate our communication with them? Should we set up a monthly meeting with that department to share progress? Can we pick a time to do an update?

I think it's best to talk with them in person: an e-mail can slip by or get deleted without being read.

Knowing how our project is progressing should help them plan ahead, and it would definitely help us reduce risk.

If the same person is on their work group and on our project team, coordination gets simpler.

Let's put a few activities in the plan at points where we need to touch base and track changes.

Perfect Phrases to Identify Who Is Going to Make the Product/Deliverable

Is there any part of this project that could trigger a "make or buy" decision?

If we have a work breakdown structure (WBS) in place, what are the main product deliverables?

Which ones have to be completed first?

Are there dependencies among our products? Which ones must we have available or in place before we can start the next one?

Who typically develops this kind of a product? Do you think we can get them on the project?

Do we know the specialized skills we need to create those deliverables? Where can we find out?

● Make sure for each one of those deliverables we have identified the needed skills and capabilities and that we have relevant job titles spelled out in the plan (designer, analyst, etc.).

We can tie the needed skills to our request for resources to make sure we can get the kinds of people we need to do a quality job, and that the project needs to succeed.

● What are we risking if we are not able to get the resource skills we need to create the product?

● Would we be likely to incur rework or schedule delays? What is the potential impact of a delay?

What would be the risk to quality if we have to work without the specific capability we need?

Can we quantify it? How many dollars are at stake here? What kinds of delays are likely? What would be the potential cost to our sponsor in lost revenue or penalty fees?

● If we can quantify the impact of inadequate resources, I can work to get special searches in place to get the experts we'll need on the project.

Can we take the risk of subcontracting such an important part of our project outcome?

I can talk to our sponsor and find out what I can do to help us get the key people we need.

Perfect Phrases to Identify Who Is Going to Put the Product/Deliverable in Place

Is installing and implementing the end product (deliverable) going to be part of this project, or will we hand it over to the operations group to put it in place?

If they install it and it needs work, can we assign a project member to stay in touch after the project is over? Do we need to keep the project open until it is completely up and running? Can we put a member of that group on our team?

Among the product development phases—initiating, creating, launching, starting up, testing—how many are going to be part of our project's scope and responsibility?

- If it is part of our project to get it up and running, and do testing and training, we will need to add it to the task plan and get budget to do it.

- If we hand it over to the operating group, can they request a maintenance budget to take it on?

- How do we know when we are done? When do we see our involvement ending, both chronologically in the schedule and in meeting all the functional requirements of the end product? Do we need to add a "control and monitor" phase after the project is done developing?

- Who integrates the product into the work stream once it is handed over? Does that person need to be tied in to our activities during design and development? What about periodic reviews?

- Make sure we have a good definition of a *quality* end product spelled out in our approach.

Tools for Managing Project Progress

Depending on the type of project, the project manager and team members will have to decide how they expect to manage the project, and then select a tool that is set up to manage progress and provide decision information for that type of project. Research and development projects manage team-based work, cross-training each other to fill in just in case a key team member is lost before the project is done. A high-level plan may be adequate, since the methods may evolve over the course of work. Installation projects may have lots of precedent for doing things a certain way, and they may even possess scheduling applications and control tools with templates that can be tailored to just this specific situation. A conceptual project may require analytical tools. A complex project may require integrated tracking software. A variable project may require decision support tools. A project management tool that collects more data than you need or tracks detail to the point it interferes with project work is not only disruptive, it is expensive. The right tool supports work.

Perfect Phrases for Selecting and Using a Project Scheduling Application

What is the best set of project management tools for this type of project?

Other than identifying when key milestones have been met and deliverables have been completed, how much tracking do we really need on this project? We do not want to select a scheduling application that requires us to track more data than we need for making decisions! Not every project requires a scheduling application. Simpler projects can be managed with a milestone schedule.

● Where do the key risks lie? Is there a way of keeping track of them in the plan itself?

● What is the best way to track our progress so we can identify changes early and stay on plan?

If it is in the plan, it needs to be tracked. If you don't want to track it, do not put it in the plan.

We will probably need more detail in some areas of the plan than others. Can we add that detail just where a key person or group needs it? Can those people maintain it within their own group?

● How will the different parts of the team report progress, using what measures, and how often?

● We team members will probably need to track more closely than our stakeholders want to see.

● Management usually wants to hear only about changes to the agreement or contract letter.

● Division or department heads will probably be most interested in progress that affects them.

● What parts of the plan are most likely to affect project cost, agreed timelines, or parameters?

● What is the best way to report that information to management once we start work using their terms, not ours?

● Will the scheduling application we have for tracking project progress work well for this project?

● Should we disable some features designed for other types of project tracking?

● Can we issue a standard set of tools for all the teams, or do some teams need a unique approach? Our reporting points and formats should all be the same.

● Does anyone have a software template that spreads costs over the project based on a previous project that was similar to ours?

● Is there some capability we need for managing progress that this tool does not have?

● How do we plug the gaps?

CHAPTER 6

Perfect Phrases to Estimate Time and Resources Needed to Do the Work

When creating estimates of when you can complete a project and how much it will take to get there, it is important to rely on careful and realistic estimates for individual parts to the plan.

High-level estimates are usually created when the project is first initiated, and these are bracketed by the earliest feasible date you could finish if everything went right (which it won't) and the latest possible date you could deliver before the project would no longer be worth doing (which you would not propose, and the sponsor and customer would not approve anyway). The guesses about how much it will take to get there are not much more accurate. To create your target dates and budgeted costs for managing the work of the team, you need something more specific. And to get more specific, you need a clear description of the final deliverable, an agreed-on approach for creating it, a list of tasks that must be completed in their proper order, as well as the type of people who will be needed to do the work. You need a plan with defined tasks suitable for delegating work to the team.

In a draft plan, you can identify the type of people by job title or role. Once you have a draft plan, you will need team input on whether the task list and the estimates are realistic. Using team input or information from another similar project, identify the work tasks and activities needed to create the final deliverable and enter them in the proper sequence in the draft plan. If you cannot describe the work in adequate detail to estimate how much time it will take and assess the resources needed, it is too early to put work tasks into a project scheduling and tracking system. Even when specific tasks and effort estimates are added to the draft plan, they will need to be validated by the person carrying out the tasks. A more experienced person who has done similar projects in the past may provide reasonably accurate estimates. An experienced person may even suggest a smaller estimate of the hours required for a task than might a junior employee or a contractor who needs to be oriented to the organization, local standards, and the approach to be used on this particular project.

The team member names and effort estimates are revised and maintained on the project management scheduling and tracking tool selected for the project. Common tools for scheduling and tracking projects have different strengths and weaknesses. The project management core team should select the tracking tool that works best for this project and this team and, if necessary, disable or place out of bounds any features that do not suit the project's unique characteristics.

Once the effort estimate has been developed, the project manager and team can talk about how many hours, days, weeks, or months will be required to complete the project. The effort estimate numbers will then be used to determine effort costs for the budget along with physical items or services that will need to be purchased for the project work to progress. To create an estimate of the amount of effort that will be needed to complete the project, the project team needs the effort estimate numbers validated by the people who will do the work. Only then will it be feasible to determine if effort will be under the effort limit set by the sponsor. The estimated effort hours are then multiplied by the hourly cost or "burden" for each employee or contractor. Together with the actual purchasing costs, these numbers make up the budget estimate for performing the project.

When discussing effort versus duration, effort is the billable time, or actual work hours, that will accrue to the project, while duration is the calendar time (days, weeks, months), or elapsed time. Duration will equal effort when a resource is applied to the task or creation of a deliverable 100 percent of the available time in a working day (i.e., eight hours).

Here's an example: The duration of a task to create a deliverable is 5 days and a working day is 8 hours. The effort estimate for creating that deliverable is 40 hours or 5 days. If one person is assigned full time to this work, duration equals effort. If they are assigned half time, and no one else is working on the deliverable, the duration is 10 days.

The cost estimate for the project includes both internal and external costs. It is used to create an estimate of the amount of money that the team will require to complete the project. Once the cost estimate is developed, the team can determine if project cost will be under the cost limit set by the sponsor, and potentially determine what outside dollar amounts must be allocated as well to fully equip the team to complete its work.

Perfect Phrases for Addressing Effort and Cost Estimates

Let's estimate the amount of effort that will be required to complete the project.

How much effort will each team member or subproject team need to create the project deliverables?

How much effort will each team member or subproject team be able to spend on project management activities?

What is the accuracy of the estimate for the total? What is the range? [No less than X, no greater than Y.]

Is the estimate over the effort limit set by the sponsor? If so, by how much?

Let's also estimate the amount of money that will be required to complete the project—in other words, what it will cost us to do the work contained in the project scope.

How much money will the project team spend on internal costs, such as effort costs and cross-charges?

- How much money will the project team spend on external purchases, for example, equipment, materials, outside labor?

- What is the accuracy of the estimate? Can we state how accurate we think it is?

- What is the range of potential high or low costs? Is the estimate over the cost limit set by the sponsor? If so, by how much?

- Remember, if you do not have reasonably accurate estimates against which to track the project, we will be going through a bureaucratic exercise to report on its status, because the plan will not be reliable enough to use for decision-making purposes or the decisions made on the basis of those status reports will be unfounded.

Perfect Phrases to Describe Ranges of Time Acceptable for Delivering Project Results

- Let's set a target date to finish the work and close the project. It may not be very accurate, but without a target date for delivery, we won't have a basis for reevaluating the process to refine it.

- The actual delivery date will very likely differ from our target, since we do not yet have input from the people who will actually be doing the work. We many have left out entire tasks, and adding them will change the final date from what we are targeting now.

- There may be quality or regulatory issues associated with our work, and they will add tasks and costs to the project as well. And there may even be "wait time" involved while those issues are resolved. That could change the end date as well.

Perfect Phrases to Describe Ranges of Resources and Costs Needed to Complete Work

- It is pretty clear at this point that we won't be able to do the project for less than _____ hours unless we experience some real groundbreaking process improvements.

- Can we ask a couple of you to study the plan and look for ways to shorten the time frame?

- Can we take a look at ways we can do this work at a lower cost than this? What can we change?

- In a bare-bones situation, we could probably do it with _____ dollars but everything would have to go as planned. If we get any big surprises, things could change in a hurry!

- Are there any other sources of support or revenue to lighten the cost burden on the sponsor?

- What are some benefits the organization will get by completing this? Are there spin-offs? Can we quantify the value of those benefits, especially in the short-term?

● What is the long-range benefit of putting some of this stuff in place? How long will it take to break even on what has been put into the project? How long before big benefits are realized?

Perfect Phrases to Identify the Type of Person to Add to the Project Team

● We need not only technical expertise on the team, but also lots of well-rounded people! What kind of leaders will be important? What about problem-solving capability?

● Based on whom we will be working with, is there a special skill all of us should have? Language maybe? Government regulatory experience? Sales skill? Persuasiveness? Change management?

● What kinds of people will we need that are particularly hard to find? Where do we look for them? If it takes longer to get them, should we start our requisitioning and/or search right now?

● Will we need our sponsor's help to get the hard-to-find skills or knowledge we need?

Perfect Phrases to Show How Assigned People Can Affect Completion Schedules

● What is the latest point in the schedule that we have to have our key experts on board?

- If we do not get the people and skills we need by the time we start the _____ (name first task), what will we need to do to shift to other work or move some future task forward until we get them?

- Is there anyone we need who is free now but who might get assigned elsewhere if we do not put them on this team?

- Whose approval do we need to make an exception so we get the right people on this project?

- If we end up with people assigned to the project who are less experienced than we need, can we estimate the overall effort needed to get them up to speed and supervise their work?

CHAPTER 7

Perfect Phrases to Lead the Team's Project Planning

igh-level planning is carried out early in the project planning process to create the framework for the project's management. Discussions with management and documentation early in the initiation phase of a project help to clarify the need, define the final product and customer requirements, pin down critical success factors, and define the boundaries and scope of work for the project's leaders to move forward with planning. As high-level planning progresses, team specialists help describe the proposed approach that will be used to create the final deliverable, define interim deliverables leading to the final deliverable, list the tasks needed to create those deliverables, and estimate their duration. Once a work breakdown structure is established, deliverables and milestones can be entered into a scheduling application, enabling sequencing and linking the tasks, blocking out an estimated timetable for the project by phase or subprojects, clarifying interdependencies, proposing a more refined estimate of the project's overall duration, and identifying the types of resources that will be needed to create the final product, deliver the business outcome, and generate critical deliverables to satisfy the customers' need.

The answers to basic questions during project initiation have been captured in the project charter document and approved by management. These answers are the foundation for creating the detailed documentation of the project plan.

Without a confident foundation that has agreement from the key decision makers, putting a work plan into project management software requires a leap of faith. With an agreed-on foundation, the specifics of the plan can be entered with confidence, and when the plan is fully developed, it should agree with the assumptions and constraints placed on the project by senior management. That consistency, together with agreement on any significant changes that arise during the planning process, allow the project manager and team to ask for management approval of the overall plan and begin work. On large projects, some organizations have two management approval points, one after the high-level plan is developed, and another after the detailed plan has been refined with input from the team members who will be doing the work.

To be realistic and achievable, the detailed plan requires input from the people who will do the work. The initial plan, or high-level plan as it is sometimes called, is entered into the project management tracking software and distributed to the team members charged with creating the project's interim and final deliverables. They, in turn, will review the high-level tasks and estimates in light of what they know will be necessary to do the work. At this point, team-member input can catch activities that might have been overlooked and adjust the effort estimates based on what they know is required to complete each task. When the estimates are revised and all the interdependent tasks are linked together, we get the first look at a proposed project delivery date. If that date is not in line with the estimated original date ranges, then work on the plan tightens up the linkages, until the plan and the acceptable date ranges are reasonably aligned. If the refined plan still cannot meet the "drop dead" dates needed to make the project worth doing—meet a market window for a new product, for instance—then the overall plan is revisited with management to determine whether some of the parameters and constraints can be shifted or the scope boundaries changed.

Detail should not be entered into the plan before there is substantial agreement on the high-level plan. Correcting errors and making changes later in the detailed planning process can be labor-intensive and would be considered rework—wasted effort!

Perfect Phrases to Describe the Initial Plan

- This initial plan is an estimate, of course. Some people say all estimates are wrong; some are just better than others.

- It is something we can work with until we have a better way to describe what our end product will look like.

- This is not cast in concrete, so try not to circulate it too much before it becomes more realistic.

- Please don't distribute this draft version—people will get attached to it, and it will be hard to get them to change their expectations.

Perfect Phrases to Request People's Involvement in the Planning Process

Some people think planning is a waste of time because it is not very accurate, but it is difficult to move forward if we don't know where the problems may crop up. At least with a plan we have some idea which parts of the project can provide the biggest challenges.

Some planning is better than no planning at all. If there is a roadblock out there, I want to know before I decide which route to take.

In talking through our project plan we may discover some areas we don't know much about.

Once we spot an area to investigate, we might also discover it will cost a lot more to do than we thought. Better to know it up front and budget for it.

Getting more than one point of view can help us realize problems we did not think about.

Plans are just plans. They are meant to be changed. We just like to make it an orderly process.

Planning is easy up front, because changes are cheap to make "on paper." Once we get a plan management can agree to and we commit to do it—that is when I do not like to see lots of changes thrown at us.

I would rather see a high-level plan we are confident we can deliver than a detailed plan we do not consider SMART.

- The later the change is made, the more it costs to make it. Let's make changes now while they are cheap!
- One minute of planning saves six to ten minutes in implementation.
- You can't manage what you can't control, and you can't control what you have not planned.

Perfect Phrases to Manage Team Member and Project Customer Expectations

- When you describe what we will accomplish, remember, we like to "underpromise and overdeliver"!
- Can we have a conversation to verify requirements and expectations?
- Do you mind if I repeat this back to you in my own words? If I didn't get it right, let me know.
- Can I rephrase these as yes-or-no questions just to be sure we agree?
- How would we be able to measure this as complete? Is there a number we can use?
- Will we be able to compare it to an existing standard to be sure it meets requirements? Can you provide me a copy?
- Is there an existing operational definition we can use as we develop the deliverable? Can you provide me a copy?
- I just want to be sure there is no variation between what you mean when you use that phrase and how one of the team members might interpret it.

Perfect Phrases to Elicit Sponsor and Management Input into the Plan

- Let's take a look at the project charter and make sure we have the right wording.

- How often do you want to be updated on project progress?

- How much detail do you want in your briefings? One manager said, "Don't tell me about it unless it changes our agreements." Is that too little information for you?

- Here is the status report format we usually use. Does that work for you?

Requesting Changes from Project Team Members

A review of the plan that has been entered into the project tracking software helps to balance the expectations for quality and performance in the final product or deliverable with the time and resources allocated for completion. Once team members have been identified, assigned to the project, and given roles on the team, they need to review and verify the parts of the project they will be expected to perform. If they do not believe the effort estimates are reasonably achievable, they will be hesitant to commit to their due dates and deadlines. Once they review their assignments and confirm they are reasonable, they will be able to start work with confidence.

Team member names are assigned to specific tasks in the project management software. Members of the team are asked to look at the estimates and recommend changes necessary to reflect the actual work they will be doing, including the time each activity and task will require and the other people besides themselves who will need to be involved. Lengthening or shortening certain tasks can affect the sequence of work or the smooth transitions among dependent tasks, so the overall schedule must be reviewed at the detail plan level.

Perfect Phrases to Request Team Input to the Task Plan

- During detailed planning we took the scope of work, objectives, approach, and parameters already defined for the project and used them to articulate the work breakdown structure (WBS). Now that we are involved in detailed planning, I would like each team member to examine and validate what is in the plan.

- If any tasks do not appear necessary, you can recommend we discard them. Our preliminary assumptions made during project initiation may have been incorrect.

- Feel free to make changes to activities that you will be carrying out. Some of the decisions we have made since this was created have made some of them unnecessary.

- Other activities may take longer than we estimated because you have more knowledge about what the actual work entails.

Once this review is complete, I expect we will have a plan we can carry out and realistic effort and duration estimates that are accurate enough to track progress. Please take a look at the assignments that carry your name, and make any obvious corrections.

I hope to have your changes by _____ ("X" date) so we can issue a revised plan by _____ ("Y" date).

Perfect Phrases to Confirm with the Team That Work Tasks and Estimates Are Reasonable

Each team member has been asked to confirm and validate his or her part of the plan.

Please take a look at the project plan as a whole.

Are there enough activities in the plan so everyone can work with clear direction?

Is there anything that is too detailed? If we are not yet sure how it will be done, there is no sense in putting step-by-step detail into the plan that we will have to revise, or worse—track!

Let me know if you think we can discard any unnecessary items. Maybe some things are already covered elsewhere or are no longer needed.

Some of the assumptions we made earlier may have changed. We need to change the estimates as well.

There is no place on the planet you can plant a tomato and eat it on your salad in less than six to eight weeks! What do you think is the minimum time for a task, and is that time adequate?

If you are not comfortable you can do it in the time we have associated with that task, speak up now! Better to increase the estimate now than overrun the estimate later.

If we make a change here, will everything else stay the same or do we need adjustments?

The more accurate we are now, the better we will fare when we report progress.

Unless you let me know otherwise, this is the plan we will work with on the project.

Perfect Phrases to Add Refined Personnel Costs and Material Costs to the Project Budget

When we estimated what this would cost to start with, we did not have the real numbers of people and materials blocked out. We now have specific people assigned to the tasks and know their cost rates. Some of them have identified things we overlooked, and these have been added to the task plan. Is it safe to say the costs have probably gone up since then?

How should we proceed in getting a more realistic number into the budget?

How does the project cycle—the dates when we think we can start and end work—line up with the organization's budget cycle? Will the project costs be partly in one budget year and partly in another?

Even if the budget does not rely on detailed cost estimates, we need to track costs to keep them reasonable within the project itself. Otherwise we will not be able to spot and correct problems.

We approved this project based on the return on investment (ROI) being better than the cost and resources it would take to get it done. We can't calculate ROI if we can't calculate costs.

Even if they are not 100 percent accurate, we still need to understand the real personnel and material costs and put them into the plan. Who is the best person to help us quantify our personnel costs with these time estimates? Who knows the cost of the materials we have identified as needed?

Do we have records of what others have spent to do something like this?

What if external changes shift our projections?

Once we have our personnel and material cost estimates in the plan and can estimate the time it will take, we can start to talk about "on time and on budget."

● Is it more important to do everything we said was within the scope of the project, or is it more important to stay within the budget?

If we are faced with hard choices, what is most important—staying in budget, being on time, or maintaining high quality and performance?

- Does our customer agree on which gets priority if we have to choose?

- If we find out it will take a lot more money to do it all, what do you want us to do?

- If we have to, we can look for slack in the schedule or find concurrent areas of work that can run in parallel to shorten the time frame to get it done.

- Are there any areas where we can decide whether we "make or buy" what we need?

- Can we move any part of this to another project and possibly do it later?

- If time and budget are firm, can we reduce the scope of work by eliminating anything—perhaps special features or functions the customer of the project does not absolutely have to have?

Perfect Phrases to Create a Procurement Plan for the Project

- Let's determine which items are needed for doing the work and arrange to place orders.

- We need adequate lead time when ordering to be sure the materials are ready when we are.

- Will the things we need have to be purchased, or do we have existing materials we can use? Do they have to be requisitioned?

● If we use our suppliers, are the suppliers qualified to provide the specialized items we need for this project? We are not doing things the way we always do them.

Perfect Phrases to Create a Communication Plan for the Project

● We will need to identify the audiences for our project communications and the messages we think they will need to hear.

● What do you want people to know about the project when we start out?

● What do you think they will expect to hear from us?

● What types of communications should we issue from the project team? How often?

● How can we test the effectiveness of the communications we send out? Can we include ourselves in the transmission so that we receive it through the same channels and can react to it the same way others will?

Perfect Phrases to Create an Organizational Change Management Plan for the Project

● We will need a way to assess the receptiveness of the environment we will be working in and the risks associated with that environment.

- If anything needs to change in the way the organization handles these areas, we want to be sure the change really happens and that it stays that way, for the safety of the team.

- We will also need to develop a plan to sustain changes that are intended after we put our final product (service, deliverable) in place. If it is the same environment as before, our results may be rejected as unnecessary or irrelevant, or even sabotaged by someone who likes things to work the old way.

- It is probably a good idea to be sure these approaches coordinate with our communication plan, since we will want all of our messages to be consistent with supporting the new way of doing things.

- Who is responsible for managing change in the organization today?

- Is the plan feasible in this environment?

- Are there risks to our project's overall success in the way things operate here?

- Has the risk assessment been performed for launching a project like this? Who did it and where can we view the results?

Perfect Phrases to Create a Project-Level Change Management Plan

- We will have to watch to be sure our own team members don't allow unauthorized or unapproved changes in the plan. We do not need "scope creep."

● When we make a formal decision to change something—in either the product or service our project will produce, or the way we do our project work—we want it to be formally released to the team, properly identified, and the plan "up" and ready to use.

How will requests for changes be made? How are people going to submit them to the project team? How will those requests be analyzed?

Some changes may not be valid, and we need a way to reject them gracefully.

Some changes may be valid but will affect other parts of the plan.

How will the team track the status of changes that have been made so they are orderly and not too many changes are added at once?

I think we need to create a process for managing requests for changes to the project management plan.

Who on the team would be a good person to do project change management? For the project schedule and plan, it is the person who updates them.

Given what we are developing for our client or customer, the technical team should have a person formally designated to handle change management.

We might use a contractor for this role.

There will need to be management maintenance of the plan as well. We may want to analyze the pattern of expenditures for managing cash flow, adjust resource costs across the board if salaries change, build cost flexibility into some of the contracts, and so on.

These changes don't affect the team as much as they affect our agreement with our management sponsor—and possibly customer cost estimates.

Discussing the objectives again when we present the plan is a good way to verify project objectives are clear from the beginning.

It wouldn't be good to find out later in the project that we were looking at the same words but they were thinking something different than we were!

Perfect Phrases for Addressing Project Risk

OK, let's talk about what could go wrong.

● What ideas does the team have for preventing potential problems from occurring?

Who will be responsible for implementing each risk response? Which risks should we review with our sponsor?

● Which risk responses should be included in the project management plan?

How confident does the team feel about meeting project objectives?

What might prevent the team from being able to produce the final deliverable(s) according to the customer's acceptance criteria?

- What might prevent the team from being able complete the project by the project deadline?

- What might prevent the team from being able to complete the project within the project cost limits?

Perfect Phrases for Creating the Project Risk Management Plan

- Every project entails some risk. Some projects are more risky than others.

- I consider this project a high-risk (medium-risk, low-risk) project.

- We take on some risk just because the project is doing things that have not been done before or things we have not previously experienced.

- If we can quantify risk, and discuss how it will be handled, we can prepare in advance to handle risks—in case they actually turn into problems.

- The list of risks and how we will potentially respond can be added to the project management plan. We can do the thinking now and refer quickly to our defined responses when we need to. We could call it our Plan B.

- We should assess the team's ability to meet project objectives.

- The project's risk level is a quantified rating on the amount of risk we will be facing that the project objectives won't be met. We can use a standard number for high, medium, and low for each risk, then add them and divide by the number of items. That is our risk level.

● We can also assess the risk we have that we will not be able to deliver "on time and on budget."

● Having a number to discuss project risk level makes it easier to talk about risk objectively.

When we quantify the project's risk level, our sponsor (and maybe our customer?) can recommend ways to handle risk for the entire project. They do have a vested interest!

The project's risk level is determined by the risk analysis.

We can create a list of project objectives and then perform a separate analysis for each one. We can then combine them into one general project risk analysis.

The whole team can help develop a list of potential project risk events with preplanned ways to respond if those risks should materialize.

What is a project risk event? A project risk event is a potential event that impacts project objectives. The effect could be either positive or negative.

The ways we might respond can be listed for each risk. If it materializes, we use the response. It's very efficient, and we won't have to spend so much time thinking about it.

● List the risks you can identify related to the work you will be doing, and put a number on it. Keep it simple when ranking risks (1 = low, 10 = high).

When we add all the risks, the total is quite revealing.

- We don't have to list all potential risks in our risk plan, just the key risks.

- Once we have a list of risks, we can add a potential risk response for each risk.

- Risk responses are just ways to respond to risk events. We can accept, avoid, mitigate, or transfer the risk.

- When we get a list of primary risks with potential responses, we then include them in the project management plan under the title "risk management plan."

- Does our organization have standard project risk definitions? All projects have some risk, and in our organization there are some that are pretty predictable.

Perfect Phrases for Assembling the Plan and Preparing to Begin Work

- It is time to assemble the whole plan so we can begin to use it.

- The project manager and scheduling specialist can work together to compile the entire project management plan, review it, and distribute it to the team for comment.

- Team members can look for errors or inaccuracies, and once refined, we can ask for the team's approval of the plan. They need to think it is pretty good because that is what they will be working with once we get started.

- Of course, we will need to confirm that team member estimates are reasonable.

- Once we have checked it for overall accuracy we can submit the plan for approval to our management sponsor.

- Have you included an executive summary in the plan? We will need it to submit the plan for approval. Also, an executive summary is good for use with the customer.

- What kind of backup documentation do we need when we submit it for approval?

- Does the customer need to approve the plan? Do we submit the whole thing or just a high-level summary?

- Are there parts of the plan where we need customer involvement?

- Where is the best place to keep the current version of the plan so the team can access it 24/7?

- Who is a good person to take charge of the files?

CHAPTER

8

Perfect Phrases to Select the Right Project Manager and Team for the Project

"One size fits all" is not a valid concept when it comes to the right leadership and capability to successfully execute a project. Some projects require excellent diplomacy and relationship skills, others substantial knowledge of the industry area or contracting and regulatory requirements. Sometimes it is important for the project manager to know the technology behind the project. At other times it is more important that the project itself be well managed; the team leaders will know the technical aspects of the work. Once the high-level plan and charter for a project is developed, a lot more is known about what kind of project is emerging, and who might be the best person to lead it. A good match is necessary in some areas, and other less critical areas can be traded off to find a "pretty good fit."

In some organizations the person who helps to initiate and plan the project is assigned to manage the project. In other organizations, the project manager is selected after the project is defined, depending on whether the project initiation process and project charter were prepared by a project initiator or project sponsor rather than the project manager.

Perfect Phrases to Define the Project Management Core Team

- If a project manager is not yet selected for this project, let's look at the challenges.

- Who has managed a project like this before?

- Does the project manager on this one need to know a lot about _____ (the industry, the field of work, the technology platform, the development methodology)?

- How important are interpersonal skills to managing this team?

- If this is as complex a project as it appears to be, we may want to find a senior project manager, someone who can handle whatever turns up.

- If time frames are critical, maybe we need to find a scheduling expert or a really experienced project planner.

- If this turns out to be a tight schedule with a well-defined plan, we might need someone who is really good at control to bring it in on time and on budget.

- Are there any process improvements or productivity improvements we might use to shorten the time frame we need to complete the work?

Perfect Phrases to Organize Assigned People into a Project Work Team

- Now that we have a lot of people assigned with different job titles, let's create an organizational chart for the project. Who will lead each group, and to whom will they report?

- If we are going to do any team-building exercises, we need a few ground rules to go by. Let's develop our team ground rules together.

- How often will we need to get together to report on progress? What is the best time of the week to do it? Monday? Friday? Monday and Friday?

- We should schedule routine meetings when they are least likely to interrupt project work. Special meetings can be held when we really need them.

- We will need some sort of a kickoff meeting to start work. Who can organize it for us?

- Can we ask senior management to say a few words about how important this is?

Perfect Phrases to Identify, Select, and Add Specialists to the Team

- Our work breakdown structure identifies all the tangible deliverables we will need to create. Will any of them need a special skill in order to get them done? Even if it is not special, are there any skills we will need that are hard to find?

Sure we have people already on the payroll with that skill, but are they already overbooked?

How do we go about getting them? Whose cooperation or support do we need to get it done?

Do we have enough in the budget to cover external expertise?

Do we have enough time to get them on board and up to speed before we need them?

Does someone want to get started on that right away—just in case?

Perfect Phrases to Assign Roles and Responsibilities to Team Members

We have blocked out the roles on the project with simple job descriptions. Can I walk through with you the expectations for performing each of them?

Our goal is to come to some understanding about the interdependence of our work.

If I had to choose, I prefer honest and thorough communication to trying not to hurt someone's feelings! Does anyone want to argue the other side of this one?

I expect you to monitor this area closely. Do you understand what I mean by that?

- Let's make sure we understand it the same way. Can you restate it in your own words?

- Can you commit to this? It's important to all of us that it gets done, and gets done right!

- Is there any area of what we have discussed that you are not sure about? Let's explore it!

Perfect Phrases to Create a Structure for Managing the Team Members' Meetings

- We have a reporting structure for everyone on the team, and everyone knows whom to report to. Is anyone uncomfortable with this structure? Can you point out what needs to change?

- How do we report progress to management and to each other as we move forward?

- For our status meetings, can I ask each of you to send me your report in advance so I can review it? There may be solutions required, and we need to spot where the problems might turn up.

- If it is a quick update, do you mind if we have a quick "stand-up" meeting on Friday afternoon?

- Sometimes it will be necessary for all of us to get together, so we all hear the same thing once.

- If we are going to be talking things through together, a meeting of 7–10 people is maximum! With more people than that, it is hard to keep a single focus or get agreement.

One-way communication is fine if we already have the answers. Otherwise, we need to discuss!

I hope to be meeting with each of you individually on your area of the project. We can set up a schedule that works for everyone. Let me know if there are times you are just not available.

All tasks must have names and dates attached to them, not just a due date.

We need to build in time to review and align things before the "real" due date occurs.

Even though we all need to deal with the nitty-gritty, we won't be reporting that level of detail to our senior managers: they'd kill us—or worse, they'd try to manage our details for us!

Who is really good at writing reports?

Who is really good at standing up in front of a group of senior people?

Who is really good at managing lively discussions so we are all still friends when it's over?

Who is good at solving difficult problems?

Does anyone have any previous commitments or personal issues that will prevent them from taking on the role they are assigned? Any suggestions for a workaround?

Perfect Phrases to Identify Other People Who Should Be Involved

We will need to ask our sponsor if there are any groups out there we need to be working with.

Who will make sure they stay informed?

Are there other projects that we are dependent on, or who depend on us for their success?

What stakeholder groups will be weighing in on our products? Can we include them in reviews? Better yet, in design and development?

Let's review the risk list and see who will be drawn in if that risk turns into a real problem!

Any groups we should be monitoring for potential changes in regulation, policy, systems?

Who could sink our ship if they did not like the way things were going for them?

Who is the best person on our team to make contact with each of these important stakeholders? We need to record this and get their agreement to do it.

Our communications expert can draw up a communications plan and put these names in it.

● We can develop a strategy for involving each of them in advance so we head off any surprises.

CHAPTER 9

Perfect Phrases to Validate the Project Plan

Changes made during the detailed planning process either confirm or adjust the overall plan, requiring changes in scope if necessary. When the scope is fully defined, the activities list is fully developed, the tasks are sequenced for efficiently performing the work, and team members have been assigned to tasks and know their respective roles, then control points and reporting cycles can be added to the schedule. Some of these are cyclical and are simply interspersed into the calendar, while others are event-driven: they take place only when a key deliverable is complete. The work schedule will now contain both the technical tasks generated by the approach used to create the project's deliverables and the managerial tasks required to manage the work and the team. The parts of the plan that address areas like risk management, issue resolution, change management, procurement, team development, and communications will have tasks in the plan as well. When the project management activities and the technical activities are integrated, the plan is ready to use in project execution.

In preparation for management sign-off on the project plan, the estimate adjustments are rolled up into overall duration and cost estimates for the project based on changes to the schedule and effort estimates generated by the members of the team, the people who know best what is actually required to do the work. The detailed plan presented to management for approval contains both the management plan and the technical plan, integrating the management activities and the team's work plan to carry out the project.

Detailed planning—when reviewed at the project manager level—also helps to create the strategies for effective project execution. The detailed plan allows the project manager to integrate and align the plan, identify the timing and logistics of adding people and resources, review the schedule to link the time frames in the plan to the organization's business cycle and calendar, adjust the schedule to accommodate nonproject calendar events, and examine the relationships among dependent tasks and milestones to select the most auspicious points to report progress to management. The alignment of the detailed plan to the calendar enables communicating with people outside the team when project events will take place.

The completed detailed plan also creates the technical-task infrastructure that allows the team to succeed in performing its work. It lays out a cycle for adequate work periods, oversight and reviews, and documents the methods and deliverables for the team's participation in project management monitoring and control.

Perfect Phrases to Confirm Nothing Important Is Left Out of the Plan

Do you believe we have overlooked something about the plan that needs to be changed?

Is there anything in the plan that needs more explanation? What more would you like to see? Is there any area where detail can be omitted?

If you identify any big risks, we need to address them early, since it is cheaper to fix something now than it will be after we have done a lot of work on it.

If you spot a problem, let's analyze how it affects other areas and get it aligned in the plan.

Do we need to conduct a "concepts and issues" meeting to be sure we have not overlooked anything? Be sure to let me know promptly if you see the need for changes, because we expect management to sign off on this plan, and then we are committed to deliver it.

Perfect Phrases to Confirm the Right People Are Involved at the Right Points in the Project

The project sponsor can tell us who else needs to be involved.

Who will be affected by our ongoing work? Should we be keeping them in the loop?

- Are there key points where we should involve a key person in what we are doing to prevent problems or misunderstandings later?

- The project manager is responsible for tracking project benefits and reporting them to the leader of the executives' broader program (program manager) or project portfolio (portfolio manager). Do we need to confirm that we see the benefits that are expected from this project in the same way?

- What is the best place in the project to get that confirmation?

CHAPTER 10

Perfect Phrases to Get Management Sign-Off and Support

Getting formal sign-off on the project plan is important because it represents the formal agreement between the person providing the resources (the sponsor) and the people using those resources to deliver an agreed-on product or outcome (the team). By the time sign-off is requested, a general agreement already should have been achieved. But because projects go through a process of progressive elaboration, where more is known after the plan has been developed than what was known when it was first initiated, changes will have been made to confirm or adjust the plan against those early assumptions. Those changes need agreement as well. First get agreement from the team, then present the plan for management/sponsor sign-off.

If necessary, conduct a summary discussion of major changes to the schedule and overall cost estimates with the team leaders before asking for management sign-off on the plan. Also confirm any major changes to the technical approach and methods [not addressed in this book]. It is best to keep approval discussions at a high level, since detailed comments can be difficult to incorporate without revisiting the planning process. After all, the detail of how the project team delivers agreed results is a delegated responsibility of the project manager and team.

Perfect Phrases to Discuss Finalizing the Plan

- Many of the assumptions we made about this project have been either confirmed or adjusted during the process of planning.

- Let me brief you on the high-level aspects of the overall project plan we expect to implement.

- Based on our new understanding of the project, does the plan we have here still make sense?

- Is there anything about the environment of the project that changes how we need to do things?

- What's not here? What is missing?

- Would this plan be clear to someone from the outside, someone unfamiliar with this project?

- Is there anything we take so much for granted that we think we don't need to spell it out? For the sake of those new to the task, we probably should document this in the plan.

Perfect Phrases to Confirm the Planning Process Is Finished

The plan is ready to implement. What are the review points we need to enter into the plan?

● When has _____ (the project sponsor) indicated we should be doing a briefing or project review?

Are there any data we need to have before that briefing that come from other tasks?

Are there any related or dependent projects we need to check on before that briefing?

When we add closeout activities at the end, we are getting closer to a realistic end date for the project.

Are you comfortable with the plan the way it is?

Can we identify any areas we missed that should be added to the risk plan?

How confident are we about the completion date?

What are the optimistic and pessimistic dates for completion (the range)?

● How confident are we about the estimated budget (costs)?

What are the optimistic and pessimistic ranges for what this project will cost?

Perfect Phrases to Ask for Renewed Senior Management Support for the Project

● As you may have imagined, the final plan for our project is somewhat different from our original assumptions now that all the tasks and activities have been added.

● At a high level, our completion date is somewhere between _____ (date X) and _____ (date Y).

● We can state at this point that we are _____ (N%) confident this plan is an accurate projection.

● Are you comfortable with moving ahead, since we are still within the projected range?

● Is there anyone else you are aware of who might need to be briefed periodically on progress?

● How about yourself? How much do you need to know, and how can we best keep you informed?

Perfect Phrases to Ask for Sponsor Sign-Off on the Project Plan

● We have taken the parameters and assumptions you gave us early on and worked up this detailed plan for accomplishing the project by _____ (date). Can you take a look at it and let us know if we can move ahead with implementing it? Or shall I just point out the high-level control points in the plan?

● Based on what you've seen, are you comfortable with the plan?

What additional information do you need, or what else do you need to know, before you can approve it?

We are ready to begin work. May I have your signature?

Can we count on you to be at the project kickoff meeting? The meeting is scheduled for _____ (date and time) at _____ (location) or _____ (call-in number).

What role would you like to have in that first meeting?

Perfect Phrases to Confirm Agreement on the Price Range for the Project After Detailed Planning

Now that all the tasks have been fleshed out and materials added, it appears that the cost of the project will be somewhere between $ _____ (low number) and $ _____ (high number). That estimate includes the cost of things in the project plan; it does not incorporate _____ (list of exclusions).

Should we cut scope, or is this higher amount OK?

● The final estimate is approximately _____ (N%) more than our early high-level estimates.

There may be a few unexpected costs later on, but I think we have been pretty comprehensive in our detailed planning, and overlap and redundancies have been removed.

● Are you comfortable with that range of costs? If not, do you have any recommendations at this point?

This plan is still capable of delivering the benefits, now that it has been completed.

This project is/is not routine, and is/is not complex. Do you expect, based on our _____ (N%) degree of certainty, that we need a contingency budget to cover anything unexpected? It may not be necessary, but it is simply a way of managing financial risk in meeting the project budget.

Do you need any additional information, or can we move ahead with implementing the plan?

Perfect Phrases to Confirm Agreement on the Estimated Schedule for the Project

When we began working on this project plan, we discussed an optimistic delivery date of _____ (date) if things go well, and a pessimistic completion date of _____ (date). Is that date range still acceptable to you?

Based on this schedule—which reflects the best estimates of not only the project leadership but also the technical staff—we are looking at a best-case completion date of _____ (date).

What do you suggest to make sure we get a best-case project environment and support?

Do you need any additional information, or can we move ahead with implementation using this as our target completion date?

Once the project sponsor approves the plan for execution—often called the "Go/No Go Decision"—the project manager has permission to assemble the team, distribute the approved project plan, and begin work. The approved plan is moved from the project planning files into the project execution files and becomes the "baseline" plan against which changes are made (change management). With an approved plan and SMART objectives, it is now fair to expect the team to deliver the project's final product "on time and on budget."

The project team has the tools, guidance, and management support to begin project execution!

PART

Project execution is the process used to implement the project management plan and create the deliverables of the project as specified in the work breakdown structure (WBS). How complex and detailed the plan is has been shaped by the type, size, and complexity of the project (scope). The work that the team does to create the project deliverables, along with a project monitoring and controlling process set up for tracking progress, are the team's way to ensure the objectives are met.

To reduce risk and increase the chances of success, project management knowledge, skills, abilities, methods, tools, and techniques are strategically applied. These are the focus of this section.

During execution, the project team will complete the work defined in the project management plan, create the deliverables, provide status reports on the project's progress, and coordinate the project with other stakeholder groups and other projects. At the conclusion of execution, the project team will turn over the final deliverables to the customer and/or owner to implement, maintain, and use. Then the project will be ready to move to the next phase, closeout (Part 5).

Executing processes follow the task and activity sequences set up in the project plan to produce the project's deliverable. The management tasks and technical tasks are integrated into the project management plan and change management processes are used to adapt and refine it. The work that the project team will do varies by project and generally involves the technical and practical tasks needed to create the product or service the project was formed to create. The project approach and work breakdown structure define how the work is to be carried out, and the product or service requirements specify what must be created for the work results to be considered acceptable to the customer and/or user. In projects that do not apply professional project management, these aspects of the project are the primary focus of the project team.

Monitoring and controlling processes are used to track progress and identify the project management health of the project. The project manager will be monitoring the team's work, the environment, the adequacy of support the team needs to do its work, and the potential risks that might prevent the project from being successful. In monitoring the project, the project manager will track whether the project status reports have been issued as defined in the plan, whether the status has been reviewed with the sponsor and the customer at agreed intervals, whether the sponsor or customer identified any potential problems that the project team needs to consider, and whether there are any issues that need to be resolved by the sponsor. The project manager will also monitor effective work methods, team dynamics, human resource management, and quality work reviews within the technical team (not addressed in this book).

In team meetings, the project manager will conduct regular team reviews of status and will identify potential problems with the active engagement of the team.

CHAPTER  11

Perfect Phrases to Lead the Project Team

When the project manager, sponsor, customer, and team agree that the plans for the project can reasonably be achieved within the range of estimates presented in the project plan, and the project sponsor has approved the project for execution, the team shifts its focus from planning the project to actually doing the work.

The project plan has been developed in appropriate detail for the type of work to be done. Management has agreed the team can go ahead with implementing the plan. The project has now moved into the execution phase. At this point the project plan is typically called a baseline plan, and this plan—whether high level for team-focused projects or detailed for construction-oriented projects—is issued as the official version. It is distributed to the team with instructions to use it to begin work on the project. Changes made to this official version of the plan must be carried out using change management. Everyone on the team begins work using the same baseline version of the plan that was approved by management. Monitoring and control of the project's progress uses the estimates and dates in that same official version of the plan. If major changes must be made to the plan, another version is released, and everyone—team members and management—begins to use that second version.

Some projects can get by with a high-level plan as their baseline if very little is known about what will be created and members of the team are experienced in the industry and familiar with the technical methods to be applied. Other projects will require detailed plans with lots of specifics. Some projects will need to carry out a series of small projects in succession if they are not able to capture adequate information or experience to plan the entire initiative in a single project plan. Anything that cannot be described or scheduled does not belong in the project plan. After all, you can't manage what you can't control, and you can't control what you have not planned.

Most projects will engage people from different groups to carry out the work of the project, and they may or may not know each other or view the project in the same way. The initial team meeting serves many purposes: it explains the project in its official context, states the goal and objectives, introduces the key players, defines general roles and parameters for the team to begin its work, and sets the pattern for creating a true team environment. There should be meetings before the project work starts to design the kickoff meeting and to prepare the organizational reporting charts, standard formats, and a responsibility assignment matrix laying out each team member's role with regard to each project deliverable (some will generate the deliverable, while others simply review it).

The first meeting needs to be in a location and format conducive to teamwork. Some projects use structured team exercises in the initial meeting to introduce the leaders, build a team environment, and set the tone for future work. Others can carry out a project meeting using digital media and online applications. The accepted methods differ from industry to industry and on the type and complexity of the project itself. Regardless of the methods used, the first project team meeting should be carefully planned to set the standards, tone, and pace of the project's work effort and to gain team cooperation in carrying out the plan.

Before the initial team meeting, some individual team members will have been notified of their assignment to the project. All team members should receive a formal acknowledgment from the project manager of their assignment to the project, as well as an invitation to the first project team meeting. To ensure the transfer of authority for supervising the team members on the new project, the project manager should contact each team member's supervisor and confirm his or her assignment. The project's team members will be reporting to the project manager during the project's execution, even though their reporting relationship to their line boss will remain in place. The cooperation of the team member's supervisor is needed to free the employee to perform work on the project with minimal interruption from line duties. Some will make a transfer formal using a temporary work assignment. Any exceptions need to be clearly spelled out in advance.

In preparing team work assignments, the project manager and selected team leaders should confirm that team members not only have the skills required to create the deliverables but also will accept the responsibility. Team members can identify who are the stakeholders associated with their team assignments and which ones will be actually represented on the team. If there are other projects that are affected by the work on this project, or that will affect this project by their work, the team can assign a team member liaison.

Perfect Phrases to Authorize the Team to Begin Work and Create the Deliverables

- Our team is now authorized to begin work, so we need to get started creating the deliverables specified in the charter and plan.

- The project management plan contains your assignments and the expected hours for completing each of them. Your actual hours may vary slightly from the estimates. Record your hours worked as you complete tasks and activities. We will review the accuracy of our projected resource estimates and costs through your status reports. If you find anything missing or out of place, please report it.

- We will be monitoring actual results against the project management plan so that variances can be understood and their causes corrected.

- The team will generate status reports for project updates to each other and to management. Status reports help us see if we are likely to be able to deliver what we said we would within the projected resource and time estimates.

- If we find our assumptions or estimates were not accurate, we can refine them. If there is too much detail or not enough guidance for you to work with, let me know. Our goal is to have a plan that works for the entire team.

It is the entire team's responsibility to keep the project management plan up to date as changes are approved.

Perfect Phrases to Ask for Supervisor Support of Team Members

Here is the high-level project plan we will be implementing. Are there any surprises?

Are you comfortable having your subordinate(s) committed to work over this time period?

● If there are other major demands on his/her time, will you talk to me before making changes?

Can you anticipate any potential changes on the horizon that we should stay on top of?

Are you aware of any other projects or initiatives that could affect our plan as it sits now?

Are you interested in attending our project kickoff meeting?

Perfect Phrases to Kick Off the Project Team Meeting

A lot of planning and effort has gone into preparing for this meeting, and everyone here is important to the success of this project. May I welcome all of you, and quickly go over our agenda?

- Our sponsor (or whatever senior manager is present) will have a few words to share with you. [Leader is always briefed on what the manager intends to say.]

- Here is a high-level overview of the project: why we are here, what will be created as a result of this project, and why it is important that we deliver results for the organization and our customer. We will introduce you to the proposed technical approach selected for our work and give you a chance to ask questions and clarify any areas of the work you will be asked to perform.

- One of the items on our agenda today is putting some operational ground rules in place for how we expect to operate as a team.

- We will need to choose consequences that serve our purposes. Some of the consequences we may need to consider are whether it is a first-time infraction, what is the position or role of the person breaking the ground rules set by the team, and the impact of public or private confrontation. We don't want to win the battle, after all, and lose the war.

- For instance, how do we handle people who come late? Do we make them sit in the front row, do we let them duck in at the back of the room, or do we hold off on starting the meeting until all the latecomers arrive? Do we repeat what we already went over, or does each person catch up on what they missed by getting the notes or materials from a friend? If we decided the group meeting was important for everyone to attend, can someone opt out and just review the notes? Do we answer all the questions in detail, or do we keep it short and sweet and dig into the details individually after the meeting?

● Should we consider giving feedback in the meeting, or do it later, privately? We need to discuss the issue as a team. If appropriate, we can always change the ground rule if it is not working for us.

● The responsibility assignment matrix in your materials outlines the various roles we will have in relation to the deliverables we will be generating. The diagram shows who needs to be actively working to create a particular product, and who will take on the responsibility of reviewing or ensuring compliance. It also shows who has the authority to decide. We will all have different roles from time to time, so respect the contribution the others are making to our mutual success.

● Let's not let the responsibility assignment matrix supersede our work breakdown structure for accountability.

● There is an issues list with a name and a date assigned to each item. Who is going to come back to us with a recommendation on how to handle that issue? When do we need to get it?

● I expect people to try to resolve all issues and problems that fall into their area, but to take on recommendations from others on how we can improve, and feel free to make those recommendations to others as well. Quality is a team effort.

● We always assume positive intentions. Avoid blaming. Seek solutions.

Perfect Phrases to Reassess Team Composition

Once team members have reported to the project work area, it is a good idea to identify from among those on the actual team the ones who exhibit the skills required to create the deliverables that are on the subproject tree, or work breakdown structure. Sometimes credentials only emphasize primary skills, and many team members may have secondary or tertiary skills and knowledge that can be leveraged. Others may have experience but do not transfer the experience easily to a new assignment. In other cases, knowledge is more important than social skills or rapid delivery. The focus of a project is on results.

- Now that you have your work assignments, it is a good idea to identify any key stakeholders [customers or key people from other areas] who should be represented on your team.

- There are several categories of personnel who will be given team membership status. Some will be brought onto the team to give their comments or review what we are developing. Involving them early prevents problems later.

- Regular team members are expected to participate fully and attend all team/project meetings while on the project.

- Ad hoc or "part-time" team members will attend team/project meetings as needed.

- Liaison personnel, individuals on the team who are responsible to cover a stakeholder group or another project, will gather and distribute structured, proactive, and targeted communication to that stakeholder or other project.

● We should also determine whether those other departments or projects should be actually represented on your team or simply kept informed.

● As a general rule, only involve the people outside the project team who need to be involved…and only when they need to be involved!

● Each team leader should obtain the skills needed for his or her area of the project.

● We should all take responsibility to review and modify project team membership as needed to be sure we have the capability to deliver quality deliverables on time that meet customer requirements.

● Also, if any major changes are made to the project scope, the core leadership team (project manager and team leaders) will reassess the composition of the team to ensure that you still have the "right" people on the team to complete your assigned deliverables.

Perfect Phrases to Delegate Authority from Project Manager to Subproject Team Leaders

● Each of you is responsible for delivering the work products assigned to your team and supporting and supervising the individuals who create the work product elements.

- Every person on the project team is equally important. We cannot complete the project without their best efforts, and any turnover among team members adds wasted time and training.

- The structure of the team and the relationship among our work products are all blocked out in the project plan. If you have any questions or concerns, I would rather hear them now.

- Is there anything you can identify you will need—in resources or support from me—that will enable you to deliver what you are supposed to deliver?

- Take a look at the risk plan and see if there are any risks you can anticipate that have been overlooked.

- Feel free to structure your own team as you need to and work together in the best way you know how. As long as you use the required approach and deliver the products that will be ready for others to take to the next level, you are free to use your professional judgment to get it done.

- We are not interested in substituting long work hours for weak planning. Do your homework. No working "off the clock." If our estimates are wrong, let's change them.

- Any bonuses or rewards for individuals on this project will depend on our entire team being successful.

- Our success is in your hands. Let's get to work.

Perfect Phrases to Improve Teamwork

On this project, we have a team because we need each member of the team to succeed.

Every project needs a project manager, but not every project manager works the same way.

My preferred role is to serve as your facilitator (or director, based on style of management) of work progress, and that means you can expect me to show up unexpectedly at regular intervals throughout the project.

In my view, the types of challenges we are likely to face are atypical for a project like this, and I would expect each person on the team to step up to those challenges by staying on top of changes every day.

We don't have to like each other to work together.

While I would like all of you to be friends, it is not a requirement in my book. You can do a good job as a team if you simply respect each other and acknowledge the varied skills and talents each brings to this team effort.

You can't succeed as an individual on this project if you can't succeed as a member of the team.

A quality work team considers the next recipient of each team member's work product to be its customer, even on interim deliverables, and the customer would expect you to _____ (name what this customer expects). Treat your customer with respect at every level of the project.

- Some people think competition is healthy. The best competition is trying to outdo the best job you did on the last project and helping your team deliver better products and outcomes than any project you have been on in the past. Trying to outdo each other erodes relationships.

- If you find yourself in an unhealthy work environment in any way, feel free to schedule a confidential meeting with me, and I will see what we can do to make the work environment healthy for each member of the team to do his or her best work.

Perfect Phrases to Improve Team Morale

- I want all of you to feel good about the work you do, and feel good about being on this project.

- We always assume positive intentions on the part of others. Give them the benefit of the doubt.

- Acknowledge contributions, think things through, recognize others, and show respect.

- Help people feel valued. Avoid blaming. Seek a solution instead.

- We are not necessarily going to be comfortable all of the time, and we may find ourselves pretty uncomfortable some of the time. Hard work and long hours will not kill you, however.

- We brought you here because we value your skills and knowledge, and we want you to pitch in and make this project a success we can all be proud of.

We estimated what we honestly thought would be needed to do the tasks on this project, and those estimates came from both managers and team members. So they should be reasonably accurate.

If anyone asks you to work long hours outside the plan, and does it repeatedly, that is a signal that we need to revisit the accuracy of those estimates. Don't let people bury their bad estimates at your expense. Come to me and we can revisit the area of the plan that is causing problems.

We can't necessarily reward you with money, but I hope we can generate a little fun from time to time. Ideally you will learn from your work assignment and it will be useful in your career.

Feel free to work together to make your workload a little lighter. Just stay within the guidelines.

If there is anything I can do to improve the work environment, let me know. I don't bite.

Perfect Phrases to Delegate Authority from the Project Manager to Team Members

While you may have a project manager and a team leader, and even a supervisor who is not on this project, you are the only person who knows how you work best.

Within the requirements and constraints given you by this project, I expect you to find a way to give this your best shot and make it work for you.

- You are responsible for your own role on the team and for utilizing the resources and team members to support you in whatever way you need support.

- If there is a particular carrot that works for you better than just the stick, let me know. If we can work it out, we can work it in.

- You are responsible for looking out for your fellow team members. If they have family problems, personal issues, or personality quirks that might affect the success of our common effort, you don't need to get involved, but I hope you will encourage them to get whatever help they need to keep them on the project and doing their best work. If it becomes a big deal, let me know.

- We need agreements around issuing meeting minutes, agendas, project status reports, and data collection. How do we get this done? What part do you expect to do in our collective work?

Perfect Phrases to Request Surfacing Issues and Discussing Potential Problems

- I expect an honest effort and ethical behavior from everyone on the team—and that includes interactions with others who affect the project's success in any way.

- If you see a problem that is best solved by management involvement, step up and let me know. I will try to protect your confidentiality if it is at all possible to do so. If we need to involve senior management, I will take that responsibility.

- Surfacing a problem early means it will be cheaper and easier to fix than if we discovered it later on.

- When people bring up an issue, treat it shoulder-to-shoulder as a team. We do not blame the messenger for the message.

- When someone suggests an improvement, thank him/her for bringing it up. Then consider whether it should be implemented. We all benefit from quality.

- If there are pending scope, schedule, and cost changes, they need to be resolved quickly. Uncertainty can cause delays and other intangible problems.

- The possibility of change has the effect of stopping the momentum of the team.

- Let's stay focused in our meetings. A "parking lot" is a place to capture ideas that the team does not want to lose but that are not appropriate to the discussion at hand. How can we set up a parking lot to defray discussions? Can we handle these on a chart and discuss them at the end of the meeting?

Perfect Phrases for Using the Issues List

- We have established an issues list to capture, monitor, and control the resolution of issues (open action items) that arise during the project, both internal and external to the team.

- Issues represent decisions or answers that are needed in order to proceed.

- Before we created the project management plan, the issues list did double duty of tracking both issues and open action items prior to creation of the schedule. With the schedule in place, issues are tracked that may surface later as problems.

Perfect Phrases for Conducting a Project Risk Analysis

- The team will be conducting an analysis of our environment to determine potential obstacles or problems that could prevent us from meeting our project objectives.

- Project risk is the risk of not meeting the project objectives.

- Risk events can be categorized as uncertain events that positively or negatively impact the project objectives.

- We can create a list of these potential risk events and decide in advance how serious they are, and how we propose to address them. That way, when we are engaged in the work of the project, we can quickly respond and reduce delays or interference.

- We can quantify our project risk level as the amount of risk (1 = low, 10 = high) that will prevent the team from meeting project objectives, and we can discuss ways to address this risk level with our project sponsor and customer.

● Risk is easier to discuss when quantified. Here are some common terms to do so:

  ❖ *Risk limit* is the organization's or individual's maximum tolerance for the risk of not meeting the project objectives.

  ❖ *Probability* represents a numerical estimate (N% chance) the risk event will occur.

  ❖ *Impact* represents an objective measure of the consequence of a risk should it materialize. Typically time, money, quality, or reputation is at risk.

  ❖ *Risk tolerance* (*risk limit*) represents the degree, amount, or volume of risk that an organization or individual will withstand.

  ❖ *Risk register* is the document containing the results of the risk analysis, including quantitative risk analysis and risk response planning.

  ❖ *Risk management plan* is the document describing how project risk management will be structured and performed on the project.

Perfect Phrases to Develop a Risk Management Plan

To increase the chance of a successful project and to determine what obstacles or problems might affect the team's ability to meet project objectives, the project manager and team need to assess whether or not the risk level is within the limit as defined in the project charter. The team will conduct a risk analysis on the project environment, the acceptable creation of the project's final deliverable, the team's ability to abide by and finish within the defined schedule and deadline, and the capability to deliver project results within the defined cost budget.

We can determine ways in which obstacles or potential problems can be overcome by applying risk responses, and add them to the project management plan. We then communicate the project risk level to the project sponsor and others as appropriate.

Elements of the risk management plan include (a) risk analysis (we compare the project objectives to the project environment); (b) risk level (we discuss risks and responses within the team to achieve consensus on how we will respond if our risks do materialize and become problems); (c) scope risk (once we have the acceptance criteria for the final deliverable, we can perform a scope risk analysis); (d) schedule risk (with a defined deadline, and once we have a project schedule, we can perform a schedule risk assessment); and finally, (e) cost risk (using our approved cost limit, we can perform a cost risk assessment).

Perfect Phrases to Describe How to Respond to Risks

● To respond to risks when they materialize, we apply the risk management plan. It contains our thoughtful recommendation on how to address the risk and prevents potential delay caused by having to stop work to address it. Here are the categories of recommendations you will find there:

- Accept the risk: Do not change the project management plan, because there is no suitable response. Deal with the risk event if it happens.

- Avoid the risk: Change the project management plan to eliminate the probability or the impact of the risk, by the use of risk responses.

- Mitigate the risk: Change the project management plan to reduce probability or impact of the risk, using risk responses.

- Transfer the risk: Contractually or physically transfer the impact of the risk and ownership of the response to another party or another location [Insurance, Warranties, etc.].

CHAPTER 12

Perfect Phrases to Manage Project Communications

Projects rely on communication to deliver success, both within the project team itself and with people outside the project. Some people who work in project management have attributed between 50 percent and 75 percent of their project problems to communication. Sometimes the problem is simply that the message was not well communicated. But sometimes people take things out of context, or hear and remember only the parts of the communication that they expected to hear, forgetting the rest.

Because we are human, there are differences in how we expect to hear a message or what interpretation we choose to put on what we hear. If you are running a project and have messages you want to get out to people, you need to convey them well. Good communications deserve analysis. Who needs to hear what information? What is the "right time" to convey that information, and—if we expect to enlist their help in the project— what do we want them to know, and what do we want them to do with the information? First, ask why—and then decide how they need to hear it in order to do what we expect them to do. Furthermore, if we rely on communications from others in order to make decisions within our project team, we need good communication habits and processes to be sure we ourselves are getting the right message.

Perfect Phrases to Improve Communications

Always ask yourself "what is the purpose of this communication" before launching into it.

Communicating is not just about information; it is also about feelings. Let's listen for both.

OK, let me see if I understand what I just heard! (Repeat what was said in your own words.)

If correct understanding is important to the project, put some time into communicating well.

After you explain something to people, ask them to tell you not only what they just heard but also what they perceive it means. If it differs, clear up the difference before moving ahead.

E-mail ping-pong is not an efficient way to make decisions: get people together if you need to build a consensus! You can choose many different ways to get everyone into a discussion.

Complex decisions are best made with your own judgment and knowledge. Simple decisions are best made based on facts related to that specific thing. Support your recommendations and requests for decisions from others accordingly.

● Follow up to be sure the key message is still clear. Memories fade. People forget. Concepts have a way of evolving over time.

If new people join the project team, how will we make sure they get the right information?

If new people get involved with the project from outside the project team, how will we make sure they get only the information they need, and not a lot of confusing detail?

Perfect Phrases to Build a Good Communications Environment

Today there are lots of choices about how we can manage our communications. What is the best system for the type of project we are going to be running?

How do we make sure everyone has the same capability on his or her equipment?

What is the best way to make group decisions when everyone has a chance for input?

If we choose to adopt _____ (cite application) to run this project's communications, is it going to be appropriate for this type of project? Do we need to specify any conditions for using it?

What information do we want to make available just for our team versus those outside the project?

What are the "rules of engagement" for external communications, such as with the press?

Who makes the final decisions when we are approached for a public statement?

How do we document this so everyone knows and we can choose how much of it goes to which audience?

Where is the best central place to keep our communication standards and guidelines?

Who is the best person on the team to take charge of our communications plan?

● Who has the last word if there is disagreement on what and how we communicate?

Our communications plan lists who is to get what type of information, and who creates or reviews communications before they are released. Have we overlooked anything?

What is the best vehicle for reaching the different groups we need to reach?

Are some channels of communication more credible to certain groups than others?

Perfect Phrases to Develop a List of People to Receive Updates

● Who are the people most affected by the successful outcome of our project? Include them in the update list.

Who could make it difficult for us to proceed if they thought we were a threat to their success?

● Who needs to hear only that the high-level tasks are completed, and who needs more detail?

Is there anyone performing work similar to ours, or that overlaps with the intended results? Refer to our project boundaries documentation; they should be listed there. They may benefit from an update as well.

Who needs to know where we are in our schedule to prepare to support us later on?

How much information do these people need? How much information would be too much?

Are there certain channels people are accustomed to using? Give it to them in a way they are used to getting information like this, so it does not get overlooked.

There is nothing wrong with repeating something if it is important for everyone to "get it."

Perfect Phrases to Manage Contracted Workers

Have we spelled out the task deliverables for each person who will be joining the project from outside the company? Who is assigned responsibility for orienting them to the work team? To our technical methods?

Are we looking for a pair of hands to do the work, or are we engaging the smartest brain for this work? Whichever role they are engaged to perform, we treat people with appropriate respect and help them to do the best job they can for the benefit of the project.

● How much freedom do we want to give them in choosing how to do their work?

- Should everyone use the same work process or method to ensure compatibility, or is it enough to get useful products that feed the next phase of the project? Can we give contractors the standards so they know what is expected?

- Have we communicated that clearly to everyone involved, both internally and externally?

- Can we check that the people from outside understand what is expected and know the quality standards? How will they know they are doing things right?

- Under what circumstances might we reject their work products as unacceptable?

- Is that spelled out clearly in our contractual documentation?

- What is the penalty for unacceptable work products? What is the margin of error allowed?

- Who is going to check with _____ (key recipient) to be sure the message we intend is correctly understood?

- Words familiar in our organization may mean something different in another; let's make sure we have a list of key words and their definitions available for everyone to review as needed.

Perfect Phrases to Build Confidence in the Project

- While we do not have all the answers yet, we do agree on how we are going to get them.

- At the rate things are going so far, I believe we will meet our deadline.

- At our current rate of expenditure, and our projected schedule, we should do fine on costs.

- The results we are seeing so far are compatible with a successful outcome. (Cite numbers if available.)

- We have a great team of people working on this; I am confident they will get the job done as we have planned it.

- Management is confident we can do the job: they are funding our work effort.

- If we see any issues on the horizon that might obstruct progress, we will be sure to let you know. Are there any particular things you want to stay on top of?

Perfect Phrases to Prevent Outside Interference in Team Decisions

- I can look at the schedule and see if this information is already in the plan.

- We appreciate your input. I will make sure this information gets to the people who can use it.

- We have someone on the project specifically responsible for that area. Can I put you in touch with that person to make your suggestion for improvement?

- What would you like to see that would make you more comfortable with our overall progress?

Perfect Phrases for Leading Team Meetings

- The purpose of this meeting is to _____ (state meeting purpose).

- Is scope quality on track? Will the work we are doing produce good results?

- Have there been changes to the risks? Are any risks we have identified likely to develop into problems in the next work period?

- Is the project on schedule? Are we where we projected we would be?

- Is the project on track for staff effort and spending per the approved plan?

- Does the team have the right representation and skills?

- To be sure these team meetings are doing their job to enable the team to do its work, we will evaluate each team meeting before going back to work and make improvements in the meeting process.

Perfect Phrases to Manage Meeting Communications

- Wherever possible, let's use a webinar or collaborative tools instead of face-to-face meetings for our key status reports.

- We need to stay focused on the agenda. Efficient meetings get the job done faster.
- Are there some points in the project where only a face-to-face meeting will do? If so, let's make sure it is on the calendar as a face-to-face meeting, and book the meeting space.
- We plan to make the meeting agenda public before the meeting occurs, so everyone has a chance to review and comment on what will be addressed.
- Can we use a "self-correcting" workbook to get feedback right away, instead of getting it later?
- Since we seem to be in agreement, let me restate what I understand we have just agreed to.
- Are there any parts of this you can't live with? If not, we may have reached a consensus.

Perfect Phrases for Closing Out a Meeting

- Let's quickly evaluate our meeting. Is there one thing that worked well that we want to do again? Is there one thing we want to do differently next time?
- How do you rate this meeting overall?
- Did we stay on the agenda and follow our ground rules?
- What suggestions do we have for improvement?
- At intervals, _____ (the project manager and/ or other key leader) will report this status information

verbally in a review meeting with the sponsor (and—if appropriate—with the customer).

● We (the project manager and/or other key leader) will be issuing the project status report data to management.

● I will hold meetings with the sponsor and customer to review progress and anticipate any problems they may need to be aware of.

● Feedback from management will be shared with the core team and team members.

● For the people who attended, we have their comments; let's review them and decide how to use their suggestions.

● Some of the suggestions are real issues. Let's put them on our issues list and revisit them.

● If we don't act on them, just acknowledge the comment; no action is necessary.

● We will schedule periodic sponsor and customer review meetings to review the status of the project. This meeting provides the information for those reviews.

● Can we include a review of needed changes in the work environment and flag any anticipated problems?

● In our public status reports, limit the issues to those requiring help from the sponsor. Don't include minor issues that should be resolved within the team. We can handle those in another venue.

● While we are at it, let's gather and review feedback on ways to improve the project.

CHAPTER 13

Perfect Phrases to Monitor and Control Project Progress

Project monitoring and controlling is used during the entire life of the project to ensure adherence to good management methods and to the effective execution of the project management plan. The project plan, of course, includes not only the project schedule with its tasks and milestones, but also the means by which the project objectives and benefits are to be achieved. Each player in the project benefits from timely monitoring of how work is being carried out and from good control of the project. The team benefits from it as it builds confidence that their work is still on track. The sponsor benefits by getting information on how and whether the purpose of the project is being achieved, and the customer benefits from the assurance that the business use of the deliverable is going to be accomplished. The program manager can benefit by seeing progress on the organizational benefits of the project. And of course the project manager benefits by gaining information and data that will inform her leadership actions and decisions.

The essence of project monitoring and control is being able to track successes and compare estimates against reality. You cannot measure or improve the efficacy of your work unless you can compare actual results to planned results, explain the reason for the variation, and recommend how to move ahead.

A project does not march from start to finish. There are often parallel paths of work that must converge later in the project. There are interim deliverables along the way, and estimates of expenditure of resources and effort to create those deliverables. Problems can occur and work can be interrupted. Data gathered from the team can help the project manager and team members to assess the adequacy of the plan to keep their work moving ahead as agreed. When separate streams of work must converge, it helps to ensure that the deliverables are ready. Comparing actual data with what was projected in the plan is one way to identify emerging risks and issues before they become major problems. And, of course, not identifying and resolving problems can cause delays and result in overruns.

The value of monitoring and controlling is dependent on good prior planning and team involvement. To enable the team to know when it is in trouble, the plan must include a reasonably accurate estimate of how much work and how many resources (such as time, budget, and human effort) would be required to produce both interim deliverables and the project's ultimate results. If the estimates are not reasonably accurate the team will resent management control. During development of the plan, the team ensured the plan delineates all tasks required to complete the work. As the plan became more complete, the information also became more accurate. By the time the team began work, the estimates were not only reasonably accurate overall, but reflected individual work methods and experience. Those steps should have resulted in a plan the team can carry out.

The team's acceptance of monitoring and controlling assume their agreement on the reasonable accuracy of the plan. After all, unless you have a reasonable estimate of what it will take to complete the project, talking to them about delivering a project "on time and on budget" is meaningless.

The purpose of monitoring and controlling is to identify variance of actual effort, actual resource expenditure, and results from the planned work and make corrections to stay on track. Its purpose is not to control people's behavior. How people perform is a result of good leadership. Variances identified during monitoring and controlling are symptoms that what we planned isn't happening. We must know why things are not as planned or we can't get back on track. Is it poor performance? Or is it just poor planning? Just like using a map to travel to someplace new, when tracking project progress against the plan, you can't know if you are going to get there if you don't know where your activity is taking you, and then can decide whether it is still leading to your destination. In fact, your plan is worthless if it does not reflect where you are ultimately headed, and what you need to do to be successful in delivering the project's intended results. Project success is defined by the project objectives and benefits. If the objectives change, then you need to update your plan to reflect approved and agreed changes. The project plan should always be current!

Status reports from the team and progress reports to the team, to the sponsor, and to the customer capture and communicate the information needed to make decisions about the project's management. Depending on the information that is important to your customer, sponsor, and other key stakeholders, a status report for the project may include the following elements: changes to the plan, progress and status of the schedule, milestones and deliverables completed since the last update, the milestones and deliverables expected to be completed by the next scheduled update, and any changes or additions made to the risk plan, issues list, and project work environment.

Perfect Phrases for Capturing Project Status

- Are there any changes to the plan since our last update (i.e., approved/disapproved change requests)?
- Here is the progress and status of the schedule: _____ (summary).
- What are the milestones and deliverables completed since last update?
- These are the milestones and deliverables we expect to complete by the next update.
- Have we had any changes to project risk? What are our intended actions (see risk plan for actions)?
- Are there any risks tied to specific parts of the plan that are now complete and therefore can be removed from the risk list? Are there any new risks to add for the next stage of work?
- Any additions to the issues list?
- Are there any items that need action from people outside the team, or items of importance to address for your key stakeholders?

- How should we share this information?

- How is our overall _____ (cite scope item) quality? If there's a problem, we can report it as an issue.

- Do we have the status of effort and cost against our projected effort and cost estimates?

- We will issue the project status report to the people and groups who are affected by the project as appropriate.

- I plan to consult our project sponsor for advice on the areas of concern that were raised.

Perfect Phrases to Brief Team Members on How to Develop Status Reports

- The purpose of a status meeting is to check out the progress of the project, to have the team exchange updates on project progress, to monitor the environment and anticipate problems, and to review changes that are requested or required.

- We will use the status reports from the meeting to create a project status report for the sponsor, customer, and other stakeholders.

- If there are pending scope, schedule, and cost changes, they need to be resolved quickly. Uncertainty can cause delays and other intangible problems.

- Team meetings to review project status are typically scheduled at regular intervals. Look at the time frame since the last status report until the next one to project a reasonable interval between meetings. Enter that event in the project management plan at regular intervals (cyclic review).

- When the project team meets weekly, the status report will be expected to cover the weeks before and after the meeting is held. The same time span should be covered in each cycle, so the data are comparable when reviewed. Using the same format for reporting each time makes the various types of data easy to identify.

- Projects with rapid change may need to meet more often, perhaps even daily if the project environment is dangerous or in flux.

- Status reporting helps us learn more about our project progress, gives us confidence that other work streams will be complete when we need them to be, and thus helps us be successful as a team.

- Each of our team members learns how we are doing even when preparing the status report.

- We all learn how good our plan is when status reports are prepared and shared.

- How much tracking we do in our status reporting is based on the amount of detail in the plan. How much planning we need is based on the size, complexity, and priority of the project. If we are collecting too much detail, let's cut it back! We can simplify the plan.

- Remember, we only want to track as much information as we feel is useful in making decisions.

- We never want to track information that costs more to track than it is worth to us.

Just because we have always done it that way doesn't mean it is still the best way to do it.

The quality of our status data is a good source of feedback on refinements we may need to make to the plan.

Presenting progress to others outside the project helps focus us on the reality of our progress.

Often, you think you know where you are until you have to write it down and share it with others.

Actually, management can collect any data that management needs to manage the company.

What we report is usually not for you to use, but for management to use. We collect data not only for managing the organization and its contracts, but also for government or even tax purposes.

The better the data, the better the decision.

Perfect Phrases to Promote Accurate Numbers

We choose the level of accuracy that is necessary given the situation. Balance the accuracy needed with the effort to get it.

● We can't always be accurate but we should know if we are not!

● We monitor our projects and track whatever information will give us a realistic view of how we are progressing against our plan.

If we have only a general idea of what we are creating, all we need is a high-level plan. If we have a good set of requirements and project objectives, then we can really use a detailed plan.

Let's track our progress level of detail at a level commensurate with the plan.

We do not collect data we don't intend to use. If it will not be used by anyone for any reason, we should not be collecting it. If we do not need detailed data for making decisions, we will collect only general information. But that general information still needs to be accurate.

If we can let people know up front why we need the information and tell them what specific type of information we need, they can do a better job not only of capturing the information the way we want it captured but also reporting it the way we want it reported.

Perfect Phrases for Gathering Useful Data

The data we report may not seem very useful to the person reporting it, but it can be critical to someone who relies on it to make a decision.

If the data is not accurate, the decisions made using that data won't be accurate either.

Status data help us make projections. If we have estimated 1,000 hours and have spent 600, does that mean we have

400 hours of work left to do to finish the job? A better way is to estimate what it will take to finish the work and add it to what was spent/used so far. The new total may exceed the original budget. We may in fact have 600 hours more work to do in order to finish, and if so, we need to increase the task budget to 1,200 hours. That way we have enough resources to actually complete the work.

● If we can identify the purpose of the data when we request it, the team can do a better job of reporting it.

● Transparency is good.

● Don't try to change the estimates so they look good. Just report what you know is accurate.

● The more information we have available to us for making our decisions, the easier it will be for us to decide whether it is the right information or not.

● If we do not get enough information, or not often enough, we can always ask for more information more often. It is better to start simple with clear requests for specific information.

● Things change, even over the course of the project. Let's make sure the data we collect is still relevant today!

Perfect Phrases to Control Project Costs

● If costs change, we may not have thought of everything when we were planning. Sometimes you have to start doing the work to identify some of the items you need.

When this happens, remember to be more careful or thorough next time.

● We may not know whether we have any cushion or surplus in our budget until we have tracked actual expenditures. We should track expenditures to see exactly where we are in relation to where we should be at this point in the project.

● If we have no contingency resources, we need to track spending carefully. If we have no cushion for error in our task estimates, we need to be equally on top of our actuals.

● How accurate do our numbers need to be? There is a trade-off between the amount of planning detail and the accuracy of our estimates. Lots of detail usually means high accuracy. Little detail usually means lower accuracy.

● We plan to compare what we have done with what we expected to have completed by this point in the project. Is it going to be enough? We should be able to tell after we move forward. We can spot trends emerging and take action.

● If the project plan changes, the resources needed to carry out the plan also will change.

● If the specifications change, no one should be surprised if the cost of resources changes as well.

● If it is now different from what was specified in the charter, then costs are likely to go up.

● When in doubt, don't make changes to the project plan without going through change management.

Perfect Phrases to Improve Work Efficiency

● The resources we have to work with are people, time, and money. They all have limits.

● If we remove errors, duplication, and wasted time, we are working reasonably efficiently. There is always going to be some level of rework; our goal is to keep rework to a minimum.

● When we are doing something for the first time, it is not going to be as efficient as if we had done it many times and improved how we did it each time. Projects often are the first time. When the project is over, we will be better able to predict what it will take to do it again.

● It is hard to know when you are 25 percent or 50 percent or 75 percent complete until you know how much effort it will take to complete the deliverable. We report 100 percent complete when we are done. Then we know.

● If you tell us how confident you are that your estimates are accurate, we can better determine whether we are being efficient in our use of resources.

● We need accurate information to track detailed progress. We can specify the degree of accuracy we need up front. In this project, we expect _____ (estimated number) degree of accuracy.

● Project effort is not free. Use it wisely. Consider what is not being done on the project that is more important when extra effort is expended unnecessarily.

● They are all estimates anyway. An estimate is called an estimate for a reason.

● Define what our estimates mean, and what they include. If things change, change the estimate to reflect what is being done, once approved.

Perfect Phrases to Identify and Prevent "Scope Creep"

● If it is in the plan, it is in the estimate and will be completed. If you are asked to do something not in the plan, prepare a change request. The scope of the project can only be changed with approval.

● The scope of the work, the work breakdown structure, and the project plan are documented. Understand them and stay within them. That way you are less likely to overrun the costs on the project by doing unnecessary work.

● The work breakdown structure spells out the project's roles and responsibilities for every deliverable. Stick within the scope of your role.

● If someone asks you to do something you are not sure is in the plan, say, "Let me see if I understand what you just asked me to do." If it is a misunderstanding, that helps clear it up.

Perfect Phrases to Report Progress to Others

When reporting progress to those outside the team, tailor the status information in those reports to the audience. Example: Management likes data!

Dashboards or bar charts are a good way to visually present progress against the plan. Use numbers to present status about time, money, or quality.

Don't give people more information than they need unless they specifically ask for it. Even then, attach it as a backup to the report.

Don't clutter your reports with added data. Our reports should display status clearly using the same format each time so people can see what they want easily. A standard format enables finding information quickly.

Use the communications plan to determine who gets what in terms of progress reports.

Make sure that what you are conveying about our progress is crystal clear to you and to your audience. Ask for confirmation of their understanding, and respond to their questions openly, as needed.

● When communicating with management, use the language of management—data!

Communications regarding time, money, or quality are better received if presented using data.

CHAPTER 14

Perfect Phrases to Troubleshoot Project Problems

There will always be variances from the plan during project execution. If we knew in advance what was going to happen, it would not be a project. So, when managing a project, you need to be like the methodical sleuth in the old mystery stories. If you see something in your actual numbers that is different from what is in the plan, you have a problem! Only when you identify what is causing that variance are you in any position to solve that problem. What are some of the causes of that problem? It could be a simple misunderstanding. It could be that something was not very well defined, and a team member is doing something different from what was anticipated when the assignment was given. It could be a sequencing error. Use data to explore the problem.

Once the problem is properly identified, a change can be made to align what is in the plan with what is actually occurring. Remember, the project plan is simply a road map to keep team members from wandering too far off course as they progress in their work and to anticipate what may be coming. Its purpose is to guide the team forward, not to bind it to some contractual delivery on a number that purports to be "on time and on budget." After all, a plan is based on estimates.

Perfect Phrases to Find Out If There Are Variances from the Plan

- Our project team meetings help us review status of our work and identify potential project problems. In addition to progress on our tasks, we should also ask ourselves if our scope quality is on track.

- Have there been changes to the probability or impact of risk events? Some risk events did not occur, and can be removed from the review list. Others emerged as the project progressed.

- Is the project on schedule based on the status reports we just heard from the team?

- Is the project on track for staff effort and spending based on what is in the approved plan?

- Does the team have the right representation and skills to do the work?

- What went well and what should change?

- Did we stay on the agenda during team meetings and follow our ground rules?

- Have the project status reports been issued as indicated in the plan?

Are our review meetings with our sponsor and customer positioned correctly in the schedule to review progress with them and anticipate problems for the next period?

Has our sponsor or customer identified any potential problems that the project team needs to consider as we move forward?

Are there any issues identified that need to be resolved by the project sponsor?

Going forward, if there are any variances from the plan, let me know. We will need to find out why and fix it.

Let's reforecast our estimates, take a deeper look.

If we see something strange that can't be explained, let's look at it from every angle rather than make a snap judgment.

We always assume positive intent. If we do find a problem, collectively we can resolve it without trying to blame someone.

Perfect Phrases to Distinguish Big Problems from Small Problems

What is the effect of this problem on the outcome of the project?

● Can we quantify how it will impact the project's deadline, the budget, or product quality?

● Before we can describe this as a serious problem, what does *serious* mean to you? Can it be quantified in cost, time, or quality?

- We can express variations by stating our expectations in ranges. If it is within the normal range, then it is in control. If it is outside the expected range, it is categorized as a "special cause." A special cause needs to be investigated.

Estimates are just estimates. They are not perfect. Sometimes they are not even very accurate.

Perfect Phrases to Verify That Project Changes Have Been Included in the Plan

We need to make sure all project changes are included in the approved plan by checking it against the project change request log.

If the change affects the plan, the changes are in the change log.

Perfect Phrases to Explain Why Deviation/ Variance Happens and How to Correct It

If you have a variance, you need to know why it happened before you can correct it.

Think like a sleuth: What caused it?

There has to be a cause for what's occurring.

If we have a problem, maybe we left something out.

Did we make some sort of mistake we did not acknowledge?

- Was this due to a performance problem?

- Is another person doing the task with less experience than we anticipated was needed?

- Could we be overcharged for something we purchased?

- We can always ask for more money if there is work to do that did not get into the plan. Are we working efficiently? Better to find out now when we can still make a change.

- Perhaps our project was less important than another, and the resources were diverted.

- If a large variance has a single cause and we correct it, we should be back on plan after that.

Perfect Phrases to Check Team Guidance on Making Time-Cost-Quality Trade-Offs

- Our sponsor and customer have told us that meeting the delivery date is the most important priority on our project. What can we do to be sure we meet that delivery date as planned?

- Despite a clear schedule and reasonable progress in developing the required products, we may not be able to get additional budget if we run short of funds. What can we do to make sure we get all of our requirements met and deliverables completed before we run out of money?

- At this point in time, it appears that our deadlines and cost limits are important, but the quality of our product is absolutely critical to the project. Quality is the most important of "quality, cost, and schedule."

Perfect Phrases to Get Management Agreement on "How Late Is 'Late'?"

- We know that no schedule is completely accurate, but we are behind schedule and don't believe we can recover.
- Tasks are getting increasingly more difficult to schedule, and people are asking us when we will be able to deliver.
- We have notified our sponsor of the difficulties we have in meeting scheduled dates, but we have not received a response.
- We will be evaluated on the success of the project regardless of whether we meet the deadline.
- Can we deliver later than the agreed target date if we still can deliver the benefits of the project?
- Can we readjust the workload to shift work off the critical path?
- Can we prioritize the critical elements of the project and focus on just those priorities?
- How often shall we brief management on our progress after implementing solutions?
- Can we adjust scope and deliver the final product in phases?

Perfect Phrases to Direct Attention of the Team to Resolve the Deviation/Variance

- Can we as a team collaborate to develop a work-around?

Can we develop creative alternatives, an alternate solution?

If anyone wants to discuss the impact of these decisions on individual work assignments, I will be glad to go over the implications with you so you can get back to work and deliver quality results.

Perfect Phrases to Review Project Risk

● Has our risk plan been working for us in identifying risks and their potential countermeasures?

Were the project team and stakeholders included in the risk analysis? Was there a consensus?

Were risk events identified and discussed using probability and impact analysis?

● Were the chosen risk responses assigned to a project team member and added to the project plan? Here are the categories of responses we identified:

❖ Accept—Do not change the project management plan, because there is no suitable response. Deal with the risk event if it happens.

❖ Avoid—Change the project management plan to eliminate the probability or the impact of the risk, by the use of risk responses.

❖ Mitigate—Change the project management plan to reduce probability or impact of the risk, using risk responses.

❖ Transfer—Contractually or physically transfer the impact of the risk and ownership of the response to another party or another location via insurance, warranties, contract provisions, and so forth.

● Does the risk reported for the project include the risk level? Is the risk level set at an acceptable level?

● Was the risk analysis shared with the project sponsor, customer, and stakeholders, as appropriate?

● How can we do a better job of reviewing project risks in the future and avoid some of these problems?

● Every project has risks. It is our job to identify them!

● We plan in advance to address the risks we can anticipate—the "known unknowns." And we handle the problems we could not have seen coming—the "unknown unknowns!"

CHAPTER  15

Perfect Phrases to Resolve Project Interference

Many times project interference can be avoided by anticipating the potential sources of interference and involving the person—customer, supervisor, user—in planning his or her role in the project. But even if roles are properly defined and understood, things change. People forget what they agreed to, and changes made to the parameters of the project shift both how things are progressing and the way they are being carried out, leading to misunderstandings.

The best way to keep people aligned with the project's progress is through frequent communication, status reports, and progress briefings. Tell them, "This is where we are, this is where we are going, this is where we look to you for involvement, and these are some of the things that have changed, with the impact of that change on what we agreed to earlier."

Perfect Phrases to Involve Project Customers on the Project

● Let's review our division of work and the roles each of us have on this part of the project.

Some roles may not have been clearly and thoroughly defined in this area. Can we go over them together to make sure we are all clear on how we contribute to this next stage?

Our requirements were pretty clearly defined when we started, but things may have evolved based on approved changes. Can we go over this together and make sure we are on the same page?

Perfect Phrases to Manage Customer and Stakeholder Expectations

● Projects seldom run as smoothly as normal operations. There is a lot more complexity when doing something for the first time that would be smoothly running after we do it a few times.

From my understanding of our agreed deliverables, this would be outside our agreed scope.

● Why don't we see what is the best thing we can do to put this in its proper light for resolution?

Are there any areas we may have overlooked that we should be investigating now to improve our project's success?

● I am confident we can do a better job of meeting project objectives with your help and support.

Perfect Phrases to Resolve Team Competition

Sometimes teams or individuals can begin to try to out-do each other, or else vie for dominance or attention. Internal competition can erode morale, and can only be resolved from above. Try these approaches to turn competition into teamwork.

● We have a huge amount of knowledge contained in this team. Let's see if we can tap what each of you knows and align that knowledge for this next stage of work.

● Some people say competition makes things better, but I think that works better in the marketplace than it does on a project team.

● Sometimes it's hard to see the whole swamp when you are down with the alligators. Do you mind if I work this through with both of you? I might be able to add another point of view.

● Let's focus on where we want to end up after we have completed this series of tasks, rather than on the tasks themselves.

● We need to get to the finish line together. No individual winners here. It's not a race!

Perfect Phrases to Meet with Team Members' Functional Managers

- Our project plan defines individual roles and expectations. Have I reviewed that with you?

- Although your subordinate is expected to support the work of the team, we all need your support for the project as a whole. How can you support us to finish this successfully?

- Here is the work that is needed to finish this deliverable. Do we have your staff member committed to making sure it is done well?

- Other tasks depend on the output of this one, and the individual you are giving us on the team is a key resource to getting it done.

- If we lose someone from the project for another priority, it will take a lot of time and effort to get another person up to speed.

- We expect a qualified person for the project.

- Changing the individual assigned to carry out this work could have a major impact on the project overall: it could add hours/days of work and add costs to the budget, possibly affecting our ability to deliver on time. How can you ensure this will not happen, or what can we do to resolve this?

- Can I arrange a short meeting with you and the team member that is being affected?

Perfect Phrases to Manage User Changes to the Agreed Product

- We started out with a pretty complete set of requirements, but a few things may have changed. Are you willing to spend a little time with me to review the requirements we are working with and the impact of any changes on our schedule or budget?

- This is the problem we are dealing with and its potential consequences. I can see _____ (cite option) as a possible solution. What do you need to see or hear to allow us to continue on this track? How can we get your support?

- Would it help if I got our project sponsor to meet with you?

- What do you need in order for us to get your support for moving ahead with the agreed product as it is currently defined?

Perfect Phrases to Identify People Who Say Yes but Mean No

- This is something that has been identified as needing some attention after the decision has been made. Now, how do you want to handle it?

- This appears to be an ongoing issue. Do you mind if I add it to the issues list so we can resolve it?

● I really need to know what you think, since it is important that we get group agreement on where we go next.

● E-mail is difficult for some of these group decisions. Can I add this item to the next conference call/meeting agenda? Would you like your name on this item, or should I handle it?

Perfect Phrases to Make Sure You Have the Right Agreement in Place

● This is what I heard you say, and it means we can _____ (restate the message in other words for clarity). Did I hear you correctly? Is that what you expect us to be doing?

● Things can get a little fuzzy with all this confusion going on. Do you mind if I clarify what I think you want us to do, and get your agreement that I have heard it correctly?

● We take pretty detailed minutes, so this will be part of the paper trail. Ask _____ (name the person) if you can take another look at it once it is in the documentation, and see if you agree it clearly states your position.

PART

CLOSEOUT

P roject closeout is the point in the project life cycle when the project's final deliverable—the product, service, process, or plan—is turned over to the customer and user to meet the need for which the project was formed. The promises and expectations created during project initiation are evaluated against results, the objectives are measured, and the benefits are realized. If the project is part of a larger program, the program management office may report on the delivery of benefits and integrate them with the benefits of other concurrent projects or recent operational changes. At the end of closeout, the members of the team are released and the space is vacated. Files are stored, and the product is handed over to the customer or user. Often an operations group is assigned responsibility for the end deliverable to put it into use.

The purpose of closeout is to ensure that all loose ends are taken care of before the project ends. The complexity and length of closeout processes will vary by project, but as the work of the project is completed, the customer provides feedback, contracts are closed, administrative processes are completed, and the resources of the project are reallocated. The people are transfered from their team roles back to their jobs or assigned to begin another project. Before they go, the team is asked to contribute "lessons learned" for the benefit of the sponsor, the next project, and the project management process. These are fed back into the system for the benefit of future projects.

A project's success rests not only on completion of the deliverables of the project, but also on the achievement of project goals and recognition of secondary benefits. Customer and sponsor feedback provides verification that these goals and benefits are on track. Methods may vary to include survey questions, online responses, or verbal replies recorded by the team.

The project closeout process helps to gauge whether the project team has completed its work, met the acceptance criteria for the final deliverables, and met the delivery dates and cost constraints, so that it may disband. It also confirms that the deliverables and products of the project have been turned over to their owners, and that the project sponsor has adequate information to determine goal achievement and conduct any necessary follow-up (for legal or regulatory requirements, for example, or for an ensuing project). Use the lessons learned to confirm and/or refine the project process with customer and sponsor comments.

CHAPTER  16

Perfect Phrases to Confirm People Got What They Expected from the Project

E arly in the planning process you worked with your project sponsor and customer to describe the final deliverable— the product or service you are now delivering—before you even started planning.

If you did not describe the final deliverable in substantial detail, you will not have a baseline against which to compare what was defined with what the team actually generated, and to confirm the value was created in exchange for the resources expended to get it done.

The value of the project may go beyond just the value of the final product or service itself. Often a project generates corollary benefits to the organization as well—a new market for existing products, perhaps—or better relationships with existing customers, new customers, or more positive visibility in the community.

Be sure to consider all of these benefits before discussing the project's completion with the sponsor and customer, since early resource estimates may not have been very accurate at predicting the final cost.

Perfect Phrases to Confirm the Project Delivers Value to the Sponsor and Customer

- At this point does it appear to you that the goals of the project will be met?
- What benefits were you anticipating as a result of this project that may accrue later, but that we could assist with as we close out the project?

Perfect Phrases to Review What the Project's Agreement Was Before Execution

- During the early stages of project initiation, we worked with management to define project success.
- Without this clear definition of project success, we would not have the critical success factors that will be used at this point in the project by _____ (name of management, user, or customer) to determine whether we succeeded in completing the project as they expected.
- We have completed all the work we said we would do, and we are ready to finish our tasks.

● Can we take some time now to go over our agreed-on scope and confirm completion?

● Typical objectives for projects that can be quantified are
  ❖ Scope/Deliverable + Acceptance Criteria
  ❖ Time/Schedule + Deadline
  ❖ Cost/Cost Estimate + Cost Limit
  ❖ Effort/Effort Estimate + Effort Limit

● Let us show you how we met the project objectives.

Perfect Phrases to Get Final Sign-Off from the Customer and Verify Acceptance

Get the customer to sign off on receipt and acceptance of the final product before you end the project. If you cannot obtain acceptance of the product, service, or outcome of the project from the customer or operations group when you complete the work, you are not "done" and will not be able to close out the project and send team members back to their regular job (or the next project).

The definition of a completed final deliverable was created early in the project planning process. If you did not record this information, you will have a hard time deciding whether the product or outcome of the project is "done." If you did not have those critical success factors before you began to plan or staff the project, you will find it extremely difficult to "redesign" the outcome to meet the satisfaction of the stakeholders.

Perfect Phrases to Confirm Product Acceptance

● Let's have a short meeting to go over what you are receiving and what we agreed to do when we began this project. If there are any discrepancies, I am confident we can work to satisfy you that we are ready to turn over the product.

● According to what you have reviewed, can we say we met the final deliverable acceptance criteria and that you are accepting the product of the project as its owner after the project is closed?

● Have we met the delivery date as agreed (or as changed by mutual agreement)?

● Were the final costs of $ _____ (cite final costs) within the approved budget (or as altered by mutual agreement)?

Perfect Phrases to Hand Over Responsibility for Deliverables

● According to our project charter and responsibilities, it was our project team's responsibility to _____ (cite scope statement) and then turn it over to you, _____ (cite specified state for deliverable), to complete the _____ (cite deliverable). Do you want to set up a time to discuss how we should carry it out?

● When we close the project, many of the people who were on the project team will be going back to their regular jobs (or on to their next project). Shall we do a thorough walk-through so we can identify if any special expertise is needed after we hand it off to you, and how that might be addressed?

● After we close the project, _____ (name of person and title or location) will be the key contact for any information about the project. Can I provide you with the contact information now, so you will have it later?

● Do you have any suggestions that might improve our project management process? Was it effective? Did we keep you well informed, and were our customer review meetings effective? Were our communications complete, adequate, and clear?

● Was management supportive of the project, and did our project plan work well?

● Any other suggestions for improvement that might benefit future project teams?

● The project closeout report is our final project status report. We will state in it what was created and where it will be after the project is over.

● If we have any improvements in the project management processes, we put them into the Lessons Learned file for future teams.

Perfect Phrases to Celebrate Project Closeout

● As of this date _____ (cite date), the _____ (cite team name or group) will be completing its work on the _____ (cite deliverable name) and turning responsibility for _____ (cite deliverable name) over to _____ (recipient group or authority) who will assume control over the _____ (scope of use of what is being delivered).

● The following people were on the project team and contributed to its success (name them).

● Let's have a party!

Perfect Phrases for Capturing Improvements for Future Projects

Before you close the project, assemble the team and talk about how the project went. Record suggestions for improvement and pass them on. If you have no mechanism for capturing "lessons learned" on the project and feeding them into the systems and processes of the next project, the next project may not be any more successful than this project was. Even if you are fortunate enough to get the same talent on the next team, often the same mistakes are repeated.

Perfect Phrases for Gathering Lessons Learned Regarding the Product

● Let's discuss some of the lessons we learned from this project that can help the people who maintain the _____ (cite name of final deliverable) after the project is over.

● First, what are some of the things you think we did particularly well, and should do again? Are there specific technical methods or development approaches that were successfully applied and might be applied in the future?

● Can we identify things we could have done differently that might have made our effort easier?

● What were some of the unexpected things that interfered with performing the work and creating the deliverables as planned?

● Were our resources adequate and did we get the support we needed in a timely way?

● Are there any specific characteristics about the _____ (cite deliverable) that we can communicate to the _____ (name of recipient group) that will improve its use or enhance its benefits?

Perfect Phrases for Gathering Lessons Learned Regarding the Process

● Do you think our project process could be improved? What improvements might we recommend to anyone doing this type of thing again?

● Where is the best place to record these changes so people can access them early in the process?

● Anything else you might recommend we record for future teams?

● Let's take a look at what worked well—or what might we change—in each phase of the project life cycle (initiation, planning, execution, or closeout)?

Did each life cycle process work well in preparing us for moving into the next phase of the life cycle? Was the charter adequate? Was the plan detailed enough or too detailed? Was our execution of the plan adequate for the team to progress in its work? Were changes handled effectively? Did the hand-off of the product go as it should? Are we ready to close the project and move on?

Overall, how successful were we in meeting the goals established for this project?

Would people outside the team see it differently?

Any improvements you would suggest for our quality plan? Our risk analysis? Our procurement plan? Our change management plan? Our communications plan? Our cost management?

Any comments on team membership? How our human resources were managed?

● Does anyone deserve special recognition? What is the best way to recognize good performance for team members?

What can you recommend as lessons learned for the next project similar to this one?

Good luck on your new assignment!

APPENDIX

Glossary

This section contains definitions common to project management used in conformance with the *PMBOK® Guide*, Fourth Edition, published by the Project Management Institute, Newtown, Pennsylvania, and related documents. Some of the definitions have been adapted from practice.

The Project Life Cycle: Processes

Project initiation   Project initiation is a process that can result in the authorization of a new project, if the basic information captured in the project charter is approved.

Project planning   Project planning is a process used to develop the project management plan. Planning also identifies the technical and managerial tasks detailing how the final product of the project will be created as well as how the project work will be executed, monitored, and controlled. The plan helps guide the work of the project team once approved for execution.

Project execution   Project execution is a process that can result in the creation of the project's final deliverable and the delivery of project value and stakeholder benefits.

Monitoring and controlling Monitoring and controlling is the process of tracking and reviewing the plan, and monitoring project progress to ensure the project objectives are met, taking corrective action when needed.

Project closeout Project closeout is the process of finalizing the project to ensure that all project work is complete and that the project has met its objectives, and issuing a project closeout report.

Definitions of Terms Used in This Book

Acceptance criteria (for deliverables) Acceptance criteria are used by the customer to judge whether or not he/she is satisfied with the final deliverable. Acceptance criteria should be defined in objective and specific terms so there is no question what the customer expects.

Closure Closure is the word used to describe completing a key process in order to move to the next sequential process. Processes occur at every phase of the project management life cycle.

Create the deliverables Creating the deliverables is a process that results in the technical products, services, or results of the project and any interim products that ultimately produce the project's value or result. Project deliverables are created during the project's execution phase. Project management deliverables are created during the entire project life cycle.

Deliverable A deliverable is any unique and verifiable product, result, or capability to perform a service that must be produced to complete a process, phase, or project, whether final or interim.

Deliverables/interdependent schedule An interdependent schedule is a flowchart or a diagram of the work of the project—deliverables and/or activities— in the logical order that the work is planned with predecessors identified for each deliverable.

Earned value   Earned value compares the value of the completed work with the budget (money and/or effort) and schedule used to complete that work, to objectively measure project performance and progress.

Lessons Learned   The improvements and lessons learned by the project team are captured and recorded for later use. Lessons learned are recorded throughout the project and filed on closure.

Milestone schedule   A summary-level schedule that identifies the major schedule milestones—significant points in the project—is a milestone schedule.

Milestones   Milestones are key events or significant points in the project.

Monitor and control   Monitoring is the process of tracking and reviewing project progress to ensure the project objectives are met, and controlling is taking corrective action when needed.

Program   A program is a group of related projects managed in a coordinated way to obtain benefits and control not available from managing them individually. Programs may include elements of related work outside of the discrete projects in the program.

Project   A project is a temporary endeavor undertaken to create a unique product, service, or result (deliverables).

Project charter   A project charter is a document that describes what is expected from the project team by the project sponsor and/or customer and establishes the assumptions, constraints, and limitations within which the project team will work to create the project's end deliverable.

Project closeout report   The project closeout report summarizes the project results: what was created and the disposition of the final project deliverables; any improvements identified as needed in the project management processes; and the lessons learned for the benefit of future project teams.

Project cost   Project cost is the amount of money (budgeted or spent) to complete the project.

Project customer   The project customer is the person or group that accepts or approves the deliverable(s), provides requirements for the deliverable on behalf of the user, or is the user of the end deliverable.

Project effort   Project effort is the amount of human resources required (budgeted or spent) to complete the project.

Project management   Project management is the application of knowledge, skills, tools, and techniques to project activities to meet the project requirements.

Project management life cycle   A series of four phases comprise the life cycle of a project from the management perspective, from its beginning when the effort is first identified as a potential project (initiation), to planning the project at a high level and in detail (planning), to the work phase to create the deliverables, monitoring work and controlling variances (execution), to its dissolution upon closure of all contracts and obligations (closeout). The output of one phase provides the input to the next phase; the phases are sequential and consecutive. When the last phase (project closeout) ends, the project is over.

Project management plan   The plan is usually prepared by the project manager and the project team; contains detail on how the project will be executed, monitored, and controlled; usually contains information on risk, schedules, deliverables, resources, and cost. The project plan includes both the project management plan and the plan that is used to create the product, service, or result. The management plan and technical plan are integrated and managed together.

Project procurement plan When applicable, the project procurement plan identifies the strategy, requirements, and schedule needed to purchase or acquire the products, services, or results needed from outside the project team at the appropriate time to perform the work.

Project risk Project risk is the risk of not meeting project objectives. Risks are uncertain events that can positively or negatively impact project objectives, such as deliverables/scope, deadlines/schedule, budget/cost, budget/effort and quality.

Project Risk Analysis Project risk analysis contains obstacles or problems that could prevent the project from meeting the project objectives and includes deliverables and/or tasks that can mitigate or prevent the project risks. These responses to risks are included in the project plan.

Project schedule The planned dates for performing scheduled activities and the planned dates for meeting scheduled milestones comprise the project schedule.

Project Sponsor The project sponsor is the person accountable to meet project objectives and to provide project oversight. The project sponsor may also be called the project champion. Typically the project sponsor represents management, initiates the project, breaks barriers to team progress, and provides support to the project.

Project Team A project team is generally comprised of the project manager, project management team, team leaders, and team members who carry out the work.

Project team members A project team is comprised of members with specific knowledge and skill to complete the project:

the project manager, project management team, and team leaders with relevant technical or industry knowledge. Other team members who carry out the work are assigned to the project to create specific deliverables, or to perform a defined function and they are accountable for their deliverables. Some large projects have multiple project teams, each with their own leadership.

Project team membership Project team membership bestows group status and enables participation; it may be conferred on key stakeholders such as customer representatives or group liaisons who are not formal members of the project team.

Project status report A project status report defines the current and actual progress, explains variances from the project plan, and identifies problems and any needed corrective action. Project status reports are issued at regular intervals, usually weekly or biweekly, to keep the project on track.

Risk Response/Countermeasure Risk Responses are actions/deliverables that respond to project risk. Risk responses can be categorized as: accept, avoid, mitigate, or transfer.

Transfer Risk Repsonse Contractually or physically—the impact of the risk and ownership of the response to another party (e.g., buy insurance) or another location (headquarters).

Work Breakdown Structure A diagram or outline that describes each component in the work breakdown structure is referred to as the WBS. The WBS is usually organized by subproject with additional detail as needed, including the person accountable to do the work, the final and interim deliverables, and activities. See Figure A.1.

Project Name	Subproject Name	Subproject Final Deliverable(s)	Subproject Interim Deliverables
	Recruitment Tony	List of Applicants for Selection	Selection Criteria Approved
			Application Form Approved
			Recruitment Program Designed
			Recruitment Program Implemented
	Selection Gloria	Notified Leaders	Selection Process Designed
			Selection Leaders
	Training Valerie	Trained Leaders	Leader Strengths Identified
			Training Needs Identified
			Training Resources Identified
Community Leasership Development Project	Placement Ralph	Placed Leaders	Selected Mentors
			Leader Interest Assessment
			Matched Mentors/Leaders
			Mentored Leaders
			Community Assignments Finalized
	Donor Acquisition Lauren	200 LLG New Donors	LLG Community Awareness Program Designed
			LLG Kick-Off Dinner
			LLG Community Awareness Program Implemented
			LLG Closing Dinner
			LLG Donor Mail completed
	Project Management Valeria	15-20 New Community Leaders (FD)	
		Closeout Report Approved	Project Management Plan Approved
			Status Reports
			Project Charter Approved

Figure A.1 Sample Work Breakdown Structure—WBS

APPENDIX  B

Project Management Life Cycle Description and Checklists

Since a project, by definition, has a start and an end, it has a life cycle. In the pages that follow are key concepts in the management of a project life cycle and a checklist you can use to ensure you have covered all the main project management tasks in the initiation, planning, execution, and closeout of your project. (The life cycle of the product of the project varies by industry, and is not addressed in this book.)

The first checklist in each life cycle phase of the project is a very high-level checklist that can be used to track your progress as you move through the entire project's life cycle. It lists the key project management deliverables for each phase of the project that enable moving to the next phase and finally to closure of the project. The checklist shows common elements for most projects, as well as added elements for more complex or larger projects.

Project Management Life Cycle Checklists

The life cycle of a project is defined, from a project management perspective, with a checklist of the deliverables at each phase of the life cycle used to manage a project to a successful conclusion. For a small or noncomplex project, use the initial list for that phase to check your progress. For more complex projects, or for larger projects that have multiple groups or complex deliverables, use the later checklists as well. If an element is not appropriate in a particular project, simply mark it N/A (for "not applicable"). This list may also be used to create a tailored list for a project. (The project management life cycle for a project, its managerial processes, and their outputs are taken from *The McGraw-Hill 36-Hour Course: Project Management,* 2e © 2011 by Helen S. Cooke and Karen Tate, Appendixes A, B and E.)

Initiation Phase of Project Management Life Cycle

Check:

_____ Project initiation process complete

_____ Project charter complete

_____ Management approval received to move ahead with the project

Project Initiation

Project initiation is a process that can result in the authorization of a new project, if the basic information captured in the project charter is approved.

Process input/process output: Project initiation starts with a clear definition of the business need to be met by the project and ends with the creation of a project charter. The project charter captures management's approval and the approval of the sponsor/customer to expend resources on planning the project and specifies any constraints under which the project must operate. The project charter document also contains the necessary information to proceed with developing the project plan and defining the project's end deliverables.

Purpose: Project initiation processes help to ensure proper definition of the project and its deliverables so that the project manager, project team, project customer, and project sponsor understand the goals and constraints of the project in the same way.

Elements of Project Initiation

_____ Project objectives

_____ General description of the project's end product/ deliverable

_____ Planning checklist developed for the next phase

_____ Charter document

Charter

Purpose: The charter captures the information and decisions of project initiation in a single document so that the project manager, project team, project customer, and project sponsor can understand the goals and constraints of the project in the same way as they undertake the planning process.

Typical questions to be asked in developing the charter (or similar document) are: "Why are we doing this? What are we being asked to create? How long do we have to finish it? How much risk is the organization willing to take on? Who will be in charge? Who will do the work? What do we have to work with? How will we know we are progressing as we should? To whom are we accountable? What is most critical or important? How will we know we are done?" Developing the charter helps to answer those questions, and recording them in the charter document signifies agreement on their answers.

Charter Contents

_____ The business reasons for the project

_____ What the team is expected to produce as a result of the project (the deliverables)

_____ How much risk management is willing to accept from the project

_____ Which of the deliverables management wants to have reviewed or approved

_____ What status reports management wants to see and how often

_____ Who leads the project, and who will be on the project team

_____ The project objectives

_____ Deadlines

_____ Effort cap or limit, if any

_____ Budget or cost limit, if any

_____ Other constraints

_____ The project priorities—which is most important (cost/schedule/quality)

Planning Phase of Project Management Life Cycle

Check:

_____ Project planning process complete

_____ Project plan complete

_____ Management approval given to proceed with the project's execution

Project Planning

What is it? Project planning is a process used to develop the project management plan that guides the team in its work, enabling the team to move ahead with the project.

Process inputs: Project planning starts with a project charter (or comparable document). Process outputs: Project planning ends with the creation of the project plan.

Purpose: The project planning process is used to document the technical and managerial tasks detailing how the final product of the project will be created as well as how the project work will be executed, monitored, and controlled. The plan helps guide the work of the project team once approved for execution.

Elements of Project Planning

For all projects:

_____ Project management plan

_____ Deliverables table

_____ Project assurance (scope risk analysis, reviews, and approvals)

_____ Team membership

_____ Milestone schedule

For complex projects:
_____ Schedule risk analysis
_____ Deliverables schedule
_____ Effort estimate (range)
_____ Cost estimate (range)
_____ Procurement plan
_____ Communication plan
_____ Organizational change plan
_____ Project management plan/leadership strategy

Project Management Plan

What is it? The project management plan is a formal compilation of the tasks, activities, and other management and technical functions associated with delivering project results and outcomes. The project plan is typically formal and usually contains information on risk, schedules, deliverables, resources, and cost. In larger projects, the plan includes formal plans for communicating to the project's various audiences, and a plan for procurement, human resources management, and financial management. The project management plan is prepared by the project manager and the project team, and approved by the project sponsor and/or project customer.

Purpose: The formal, approved plan for the project not only details how the project will be executed, monitored, and controlled, but it also contains an appropriate level of information on risk, schedules, deliverables, resources, and cost to guide the team in performing work and management in tracking progress and identifying and resolving problems as they emerge.

Deliverables Table

What is it? A deliverables table is a single explanation of the deliverables required to complete the project and their inter-relationships.

Purpose: The deliverables table give the team a single source reference to understand all the deliverables of the project and the relationship of their work to the work of other team members.

Project Assurance (Scope Risk Analysis, Reviews, and Approvals)

What is it? Project assurance is a structured method to identify risks and variances in the project's progress; it allows periodic outside viewpoints on the work as it progresses toward closure.

Team Membership

What is it? Team membership is providing group status and involvement of many individuals in the work of a single project, often from various groups and functional areas.

Purpose: Team membership allows the compilation of knowledge, skills, experience, and perspectives of individuals from different sides of the project's objectives. Members are selected to aggregate all critical capabilities needed to successfully complete the project, and managed to enable effective and productive work from each member. The work of the team is often larger than the sum of its parts.

Milestone Schedule

What is it? A milestone schedule is a demarcation of the points in elapsed time when the deliverables of a project can be expected to be complete, and displaying the information to stakeholders.

Purpose: The purpose of a milestone schedule is to present commonly understood progress markers to all the various stakeholders in a project so they can assess the progress of the team toward achieving the project's intended objectives.

Execution Phase of Project Management Life Cycle

Check:

_____ Project execution processes complete

_____ Project deliverable(s) complete

_____ Project status and progress reports complete

_____ Management approval given to close the project

Project Execution

What is It? Project execution is a process that can result in the creation of the project's final deliverable and the delivery of project value and stakeholder benefits. The execution phase of the project management process consists of proactive processes to enable the team to create the project's end deliverable and reactive processes to monitor and control the variables that enable or limit the team's ability to create it. The execution process is used to implement the project management plan and manage the work that the team performs to create the product or deliverable. Project execution processes, along with project monitoring and controlling processes, comprise the project management infrastructure within which the project team generates the project's final deliverable and ensures the project objectives are met.

Process inputs: Project execution begins with a project work plan; baseline cost and schedule; refined budget; resources and contract authorizations; and verified criteria. Process outputs: Project execution ends with work results; deliverables; performance measurement documentation; product documentation; and project records.

Purpose: The purpose of project execution is to enable the team to perform the work, including the tasks and activities defined in the project management plan; to create the deliverables; to do the project tasks in the proper sequence; to provide status reports on the project's progress for guiding decisions, and to coordinate the project with other stakeholder groups and other projects. The elements of project execution ensure that the project manager and project team have defined how they will perform the work of the project within the limits and constraints of resources available, so that when the final deliverable of the project is completed and turned over to its owner, the business value is accrued. The customer applies the product of the project (deliverable) to derive benefits from its use, and the project sponsor has the means to identify the benefits the project was created to deliver for the sponsoring organization (i.e., program benefits for stakeholders).

Elements of Project Execution

For all projects:

_____ Detailed task plan and schedule

_____ Resource assignments

     _____ Defined deliverables

     _____ Project status reports

     _____ Progress reports

For complex projects

     _____ Effort status report

     _____ Cost status report

     _____ Forecast (effort or status)

     _____ Deliverables acceptance plan

Detailed Task Plan

What is it? The detailed plan for the project contains a more refined listing of the activities and effort and cost estimates for the project, as well as interim milestones, interim deliverables, calendar dates, project control points, and the names of actual personnel assigned to the project.

Purpose: In the detailed plan, you can identify the activities necessary to perform project tasks, the individuals assigned to each task, overall estimated effort and cost to do the work, refined delivery dates for completion, and the management tasks associated with the project, such as meetings, progress reports, reviews, and transitions. The work estimates in the detailed plan are more accurate than in the high-level plan because they have been reviewed and refined by those actually doing the work.

Project Schedule

What is it? The project schedule is a sequenced series of linked tasks—sequenced by elapsed time and dependency—that are based on the scope definition for the project, the work breakdown structure (WBS), and the activities and deliverables that must be completed in order to finish the project.

Purpose: To define the work of the project in sufficient detail that it can be delegated to the project team as work assignments and tracked against the allocated effort and cost budget provided for project completion; to demonstrate any dependencies of later tasks on the output of a prior task; to allocate human and material resources to specific effort and time frames; to enable monitoring and tracking progress against the plan and the achievement of milestones as interim and final deliverables are completed.

Resource Assignments

What is it? Resource assignments specify which people will be assigned to work on the project team and how fully they are released from their nonproject work to devote effort and time to the project. Resource assignments also define the financial support and budget allocated to underwrite project costs and allocate it adequately over the life cycle to enable completion.

Purpose: To allow an assessment of the adequacy of the assigned resources to meeting the project's requirements so that any unmet resource needs can be identified and addressed, enabling completion of the project's objectives.

Defined Deliverables

What is it? A defined deliverable not only describes what is to be created by the project team at key points in the schedule, but also which aspects of the deliverables of the project are needed to meet the customer criteria and requirements. The process of creating the deliverables is the process of carrying out the tasks and activities associated with the creation of the project's deliverables (product, service, process, or plan) in such a way that the use of the deliverable meets the need and justifies the expenditure of resources on the project. The tasks and deliverables vary by type of project, type of deliverable, occupational groups, and industries associated with the sponsorship and customer/user role on the project.

Purpose: Defined deliverables are sufficiently specific that the project team can determine how they should be developed and/or created to provide the intended value. The process of creating the unique deliverables associated with a given project is defined anew for the project, often with methods or techniques drawn from associated occupations and project management processes. The process may differ significantly from operations processes but may be repeated as part of the organization's business process after the deliverables are created and turned over to operations to provide the value and benefits that justified the creation of the project. Lessons learned on the project are used to refine the process so it can be repeated.

Status and Progress Reports

What is it? Status reports from the team and progress reports to the team, to the sponsor, and to the customer capture and communicate the information needed to make decisions about the project's management. Depending on the information that is important to the customer, sponsor, and other key stakeholders, a status report for the project may include the following elements: changes to the plan, progress and status of the schedule, milestones met and deliverables completed since the last update, the milestones and deliverables expected to be completed by the next scheduled update, and any changes or additions made to the risk plan, issues list, and project work environment, some of which may require sponsor involvement.

Purpose: To identify variance from the planned work and make corrections to stay on track. Variances are symptoms that what was planned isn't happening. Status reports help the project manager and team identify why things are not as planned, name the cause, and make changes to get back on track and to enable achieving the project objectives.

Closeout Phase of Project Management Life Cycle

Check:

_____ Project closeout process complete

_____ Project deliverables complete

_____ Project closeout report complete

_____ Lessons learned filed for future use

Project Closeout Process

What is it? Project closeout is a process that can result in the dissolution of the project.

Process input: The project closeout process begins with work results, performance measurement documentation, product documentation, and project records. Process output: The closeout process ends with formal acceptance of work results, management reports, lessons learned, the closeout report, and project archives.

Purpose: To ensure that the project manager, project team, project customer, and project sponsor have what they need to approve closing the project and transferring project resources out of the project work site within the constraints of the organization's legal and administrative policies.

Elements of Project Closeout

For all projects:

_____ Project closeout report

For complex projects:

_____ Contract closeout

_____ Administrative closeout

_____ Staff reassignment

_____ Process improvement

Project Closeout Report

What is it? The project closeout report captures the information that defines how the objectives of the project were met and reports disposition of the project resources. The report also specifies the location or responsibility for the product, service, or result of the project and the acceptance of that responsibility by the owner or customer.

Purpose: The project closeout report specifies how the project met the project objectives and how well it performed before the team is disbanded and the resources distributed. The closeout report also captures information on the project management process, what worked well and what could be improved for future projects (lessons learned).

Individual Checklists

Included here are individual checklists for the elements of each section of the project life cycle listed in the previous section. If desired, you can create your own checklists by identifying and copying only those elements of the checklist that apply to your project.

Project Initiation Checklists with Checklists for Subelements of Project Initiation

_____ Project objectives measurement
_____ A clear description of the final deliverable
_____ An agreed-on approach for creating the final deliverable
_____ The project charter, available for team reference
_____ Management sign-off giving the approval to proceed with the project

Project Objectives Measurement

What is it? Measurement of project objectives is a process of quantifying and tracking the indicators of success by which the sponsor/customer will consider the project to be on track and progressing toward its end results and benefits. Project objectives are a description of what the sponsor/customer hope to achieve as a result of the project and the business results that justify the expenditure of resources (outcome). Critical success factors are those elements that the project must achieve in order to be considered successful.

Purpose: To make sure the project is on track, to know as early as possible when there is a problem with the project; to look at actual results versus the plan to know when a correction needs to be made; to communicate progress to the sponsor, customer, or organization.

Project Planning Checklist with Elements of the Project Plan

_____ Deliverables table (describes features and functions of the project's final deliverable)

_____ Interim deliverables (identifies the interim deliverables that comprise each final and organizational deliverable)

_____ Project boundaries/scope (determine what tasks are and are not included in the scope of the project)

_____ Stakeholder list (identify which departments, areas, and individual stakeholders should be considered and briefed, as well as which other projects overlap/ interface with the project)

_____ Work breakdown structure (a list that breaks down the project into subprojects or work units and defines the specifics of each: subproject deliverables, who will lead each subproject, what each subproject will produce [final and interim deliverables], and who is going to be accountable for each deliverable).

Project Planning for All Projects

_____ Project management plan (includes work breakdown structure, tasks, and activities)

_____ A list of tasks that must be completed in their proper order to complete the project

_____ A list of activities that must be completed in order to complete each sequenced task

_____ A list of the types of people who will be needed to do the work and number of each

_____ A list of people available to work on the project and be assigned to tasks

For Complex Projects

_____ Specific plans to address issues, risks, contracting and procurement, team development, human resource management, communications, quality, and financial management, and tailored to the needs of the organization, industry, or environment in which the final deliverable is deployed

_____ Specific plans for monitoring and controlling the technical and managerial work of the project in conformance with the specified and agreed standards and requirements of the project's sponsor, customer, and/or user of the final deliverable

High-Level Plan

What is it? A high-level plan includes the general approach to the work of the project and key tasks needed to complete the deliverable.

Purpose: The high-level, or draft, plan for the project captures the general assumptions and constraints for the project from early management discussions, and allows broad estimates of the earliest date the project can start and the latest date it must finish to successfully meet objectives. In the high-level plan you can identify the type of people by job title or role. Once you have a draft plan, you will need team input on whether the task list and the estimates are realistic. The high-level plan identifies the tasks and some of the activities needed to create the final deliverable, but often does not contain the project management tasks, risks, communications, human resources, or procurement costs for the project.

Project Scope Description

What is it? The scope description is a complete description of the final deliverables that will be produced by the project. It is comprised of customer requirements, deliverable features and functions, and acceptance criteria. Also contains a deliverables table listing the final deliverables and any interim deliverables needed to create them.

Purpose: To document the customer requirements as well as the features and functions of the final deliverable from the project, in addition to the criteria for accepting the final deliverable. The criteria need to be SMART (specific, measureable, achievable, realistic, time-bound) and clearly defined, so the project team will know when the work is finished and the project can close.

Project Roles and Responsibilities

What is it? Project roles and responsibilities refer to the individual categories of responsibility and authority that enable the people involved in the project to work together as a team. The most common roles with defined responsibilities are the project sponsor, the project manager, the team leader, the project team member, and the project customer. These are defined later in this section.

Purpose: To enable the people associated with the project to assume one of the various roles needed to cover all the necessary managerial and technical functions of the project and its work units.

Defining and identifying roles ensures that necessary work has been assigned to some specific individual, and that all key roles are filled. Roles and responsibilities assume the place of the more familiar job description and the associated reporting hierarchy that personnel enjoy if working in a normal operating environment. There are other roles and responsibilities on the project besides these, but they will depend on what is actually being created and the industry or functional area represented by the project. The following generic roles occur on every project.

Project sponsor: The management representative accountable for project objectives, providing project oversight, approving the project resources, and the overall success of the project.

Project manager: The person assigned by the performing organization to achieve the project objectives, lead the project team and achieve project benefits for the organization.

Project lead: The person who leads a team responsible for creating the deliverable. In some projects, there are multiple teams creating key deliverables, each with a team lead with technical expertise needed to lead that team. In smaller projects, the project lead may also be the project manager, assigned by the performing organization to achieve the project objectives. As project lead, he/she has management responsibility for the project as well as technical leadership of the team.

Project team members: The people assigned to the project to perform a defined function, participate on the project team, and create the deliverables as defined, remaining accountable for the quality and timeliness of those deliverables.

Project customer: The person or group to accept the final deliverables at the end of the project, get value from the end product and achieve the business benefits. The customer provides requirements for the deliverables, accepts responsibility for the final deliverable's maintenance and deployment. The project customer often provides funding.)

Responsibility Assignment Matrix

What is it? A responsibility assignment matrix is used to describe the roles and accountabilities of various teams or people in project delivery and operations. It is especially useful in clarifying responsibilities in cross-functional/cross-departmental projects and processes. The matrix splits tasks into four participatory responsibility types, which are then assigned to different roles in the project. These responsibility types can vary by deliverable, so each team member may take a different responsibility on separate deliverables. This matrix does not supersede the work breakdown structure, which assigns responsibility for areas of work on the overall project.

Purpose: To identify responsibilities of the project to specific project roles using clear definitions so those roles can be assumed by one or more project team members. One type of responsibility assignment matrix is a RACI diagram, with each letter specifying a role:

Responsible (R)—The "doer," the one who actually completes the task. There can be several people responsible for one task.

Accountable/Approver (A)—The person ultimately answerable for the correct and thorough completion of the task. There must be only one accountable person specified for each task.

Consulted (C)—These are the individuals who are consulted before the final decision or action is made.

Informed (I)—These are the individuals who are kept up-to-date on progress but do not work on the day-to-day tasks (clients, for example).

Team Composition Profile

What is it? A team composition profile is a list of the types of people who will be needed to do the work of the project and the number of each. It is also a list of people available to work on the project and be assigned to task assignments.

Purpose: To identify appropriate skills that are required for the approach and to create the deliverables of the project; to identify who are the stakeholders with a vested interest in the project's outcome, and which of them will be represented on the team; to assess which other projects and which stakeholders require a team member liaison; and to decide how these areas will be covered—with a regular team member, an ad hoc team member, or a liaison.

Work Breakdown Structure (WBS)

What is it? The WBS is a deliverables-oriented list in hierarchical form of the work to be executed by the project team, to accomplish the project objectives and to create the required deliverables. Each descending level of the WBS represents an increasingly detailed definition of the project work, and control accounts with a unique identifier are set up for the work packages at key points in the project plan. Management can check each control point where scope, cost, and schedule are integrated and compare it to the earned value for performance measurement. Control accounts are placed at selected management points in the WBS, and work packages must be associated with only one control account.

Detailed Plan

What is it? The detailed plan for the project contains a more refined listing of the activities and effort and cost estimates for the project, as well as interim milestones, interim deliverables, calendar dates, project control points, and the names of actual personnel assigned to the project.

Purpose: In the detailed plan, you can identify the activities necessary to perform project tasks, the individuals assigned to each task, overall estimated effort and cost to do the work, refined delivery dates for completion, and the management tasks associated with the project such as meetings, progress reports, reviews, and transitions. The work estimates in the detailed plan are more accurate than in the high-level plan because they have been reviewed and refined by those actually doing the work.

Project Schedule

What is it? The project schedule is a sequenced series of linked tasks—sequenced by elapsed time and dependency—that are based on the scope definition for the project, the work breakdown structure, and the activities and deliverables that must be completed in order to complete the project.

Purpose: To define the work of the project in sufficient detail that it can be delegated to the project team as work assignments and tracked against the allocated effort and cost budget provided for project completion; to demonstrate any dependencies of later tasks on the output of a prior task; to allocate human and material resources to specific effort and time frames; and to enable monitoring and tracking progress against the plan and the achievement of milestones as interim and final deliverable(s) are completed.

Project Calendar

What is it? The project calendar overlays project work and task completion on the available work schedule of the host organization and the team members' external commitments, as well as time needed for reviews and approvals, enabling a more realistic estimate of when milestones will be met, progress reviews held, and the project's deliverables completed.

Purpose: To enable the scheduling of monitoring and reporting against the project plan as work progresses and to identify any periods of elapsed time when work may not progress due to delays, review periods, or team member absence from the project work site. The project calendar is a more accurate projection of the project's overall elapsed duration than the simple schedule.

Effort Estimate

What is it? An effort estimate shows how much effort (in hours, days, weeks, or months) will be required to complete the project. The effort estimate numbers will then be used to determine effort costs for the cost estimate (budget). Effort is the "billable" time or actual work hours that will accrue to the project.

Purpose: To create an estimate of the amount of effort that will be needed to complete the project; to determine if effort will be under the effort limit set by the sponsor; to calculate the effort costs to be used in the cost budget.

Duration Estimate

What is it? Duration is the calendar time (expressed in days, weeks, or months) or elapsed time that is projected for the project's work and closure.

Purpose: To create a sufficiently accurate estimate of elapsed time to discuss delivery dates and to schedule product turnover and implementation. Duration will equal effort when a resource is applied to the task or creation of a deliverable 100 percent of the available time in a working day (i.e., 8 hrs) and 100 percent of the working year (2,920 days). Since few projects require teams to work holidays and weekends, 2,040 working hours is usually considered a full year for a staff member. For planning purposes, the duration of a task to create a deliverable is calculated on a standard 5 days per week; a working day is 8 hours. The effort estimate for creating that deliverable is 40 hours or 5 days. If one person is assigned full time to this work, duration equals effort. If several shifts of staff are assigned to complete the work in a shorter period, effort hours will remain about the same, but duration will shorten.

Cost Estimate

What is it? A cost estimate is a budget estimate for the project that includes both internal and external costs.

Purpose: To put a realistic number on the estimated amount of money that the team will accrue and the organization will require in order to complete the project; to determine if the project cost is likely to be under the cost limit set by the sponsor; and to determine what outside dollar amounts must be allocated to enable project completion.

Project Procurement Plan

What is it? A list of items to purchase that are critical to the success of the project and an outline process for obtaining those items from many sources by the time they are needed (part of the project management plan).

Purpose: To ensure that the project team obtains the items needed at the appropriate time to meet project objectives; to coordinate with purchasing processes; to enable contracting for supportive services or equipment.

Project Communication Plan

What is it? A project communication plan is an organized list of key communications from the project team targeted to various audiences.

Purpose: The communication plan outlines the planned project communications to enable project success and allows consideration of what different stakeholders of the project need to know, how they need to hear it, and the different communication vehicles and media that will be most effective for each type of stakeholder.

Organizational Change Management Plan

What is it? Organizational change management is the application of a set of skills, tools, and techniques to implement the changes that affect people as a result of the project. The organizational change management plan outlines the activities that improve utilization of the project deliverables by means of communication, training, and deployment activities, including the names of specific deliverables, dates, and accountable individuals, as well as the management support needed to enact them.

Purpose: To ensure the benefits of the project are realized by helping stakeholders to understand and adjust to the organizational changes that are associated with project benefits.

Project Change Management Plan

What is it? Project teams need a plan for managing changes to the project management plan. In this context, the project change management plan describes how changes to scope, schedule, effort, or cost can be documented approved or denied. Then the project management plan should be revised to incorporate the approved changes. (Note: The project change management plan does not address the issues of organizational change management.)

Purpose: To determine how requests to change the project management plan will be handled; to prevent "scope creep" and to reduce risk of an inaccurate plan; to document and control the effect of changes to the project management plan. The possibility of change has the effect of stopping the momentum of the team, so addressing change openly increases work confidence.

Project Risk Analysis

What is it? Project risk analysis is the thoughtful consideration of the project environment to determine potential obstacles or problems that could prevent the team from meeting the project objectives. Examples of elements that could keep the team from meeting the project objectives are the clarity and completeness of acceptance criteria for the final deliverable, the reasonableness of the project deadline, the availability of competent staff, or reasonableness of the project cost limit.

Purpose: To identify potential barriers or obstacles and ways to address them so that the team can progress toward delivering the end product and accrue business benefits at project closure.

Project Risk Management Plan

What is it? The project risk management plan is the document describing how project risk responses will be structured and performed on the project. Project risk is the risk of *not* meeting the project objectives. This can be measured by using the acceptance criteria for the final deliverable, the project deadline, and project cost to quantify impact. Typical project objectives are what the organization has established for determining the project's success after execution. Project objectives vary, but some might be expressed as:

Scope/Deliverable + Acceptance Criteria

Time/Schedule + Deadline

Cost/Cost Estimate + Cost Limit

Effort/Effort Estimate + Effort Limit

Purpose: To quantify success and increase the chance of a successful project; to determine what obstacles or problems might affect the team's ability to meet project objectives; to assess whether or not the risk level is within limits as defined in the project charter; to determine ways in which obstacles or potential problems can be overcome by applying risk responses, and then add them to the project management plan for action; and finally, to communicate the project risk level to the project sponsor and others as appropriate. Elements of the risk management plan include risk analysis (compare the project objectives to the project environment); risk level (discuss risks and responses with the team to achieve consensus); scope (what will be performed; when you have the acceptance criteria for the final deliverable, perform a scope risk analysis); schedule risk (when you have a project schedule or a deadline, perform a schedule risk assessment); and cost risk (when you have a cost limit, perform a cost risk assessment).

Elements of the Risk Plan

❖ Risk limit: The organization's or individual's maximum tolerance for the risk of not meeting the project objectives.

❖ Risk probability: The percent chance the risk event will occur, and impact, an objective measure of the consequence expressed as time, money, quality, reputation.

❖ Risk tolerance (risk limit): The degree, amount, or volume of risk that an organization or individual will withstand.

❖ Risk register: The document containing the results of the risk analysis, including quantitative risk analysis, and risk-response planning.

Project Execution Checklists

For all projects:

❖ Detailed plan (approved)

❖ Deliverables table

❖ Status reports/risk reviews/approvals

❖ Team membership

❖ Milestone schedule

For complex projects:

_____ Schedule risk analysis

_____ Deliverables schedule

_____ Effort estimate (range)

_____ Cost estimate (range)

_____ Procurement plan

_____ Communications plan

_____ Organizational change plan

_____ Project management plan/leadership summary

Project Execution

What is it? Project execution is the process used to carry out the tasks and activities in the project plan, including both technical tasks to create the product of the project and associated deliverables, as well as managerial tasks such as those involved in project monitoring and controlling.

Process inputs: project plan, baseline cost and schedule, refined budget, resources and contract authorizations, verified criteria. Process outputs: work results, performance measurement documentation, product documentation, and project records.

Purpose: To ensure the project objectives are met; to complete the work defined in the project plan; to create the deliverables (interim and final deliverables); to revise and adjust the project work to enable completing the project on time and on budget; to enable project management guidance for the team; to provide status reports and progress reports to the project sponsor and customer; to coordinate the project with other stakeholder groups and other projects.

Project Monitoring and Control Process

What is it? A process of project monitoring and control is established as part of the project management system once the plan has been defined in detail. Project monitoring and control is used during the entire life of the project to ensure adherence to the project management plan and accomplishment of the project objectives.

Purpose: Provide information on project status to ensure that the project management plan is being followed and kept up to date, so the project objectives can be met.

Create the Deliverables

What is it? Create the deliverables is a process specified in the approach defined in the charter and project management plan; the work packages, tasks and activities to create the deliverables are defined in the work breakdown structure; monitor actual results against the project management plan so variances can be understood and corrected; generate status reports for project updates; and keep the project management plan up to date as changes are approved. The work tasks and activities that create the deliverable are spelled out in project initiation according to the requirements given by the customer or product owner and the objectives specified in the charter. The members of the team create the deliverables using the approach agreed to during high-level planning, refined during detailed planning, and spelled out in specifications and requirements. Progress in the specification and development of the project's interim and final deliverables is monitored by comparing actual reported results against the project management plan so variances can be understood and corrected. Reports on progress of deliverables is included in team status meetings; the team members generate status reports for project updates. Project change management is used to keep the project management plan up to date as changes are approved.

Purpose: To develop the end products (deliverables) that will eventually be what is turned over to the customer or product owner, incorporated into operations, and maintained and used so they are able to deliver the intended business results and benefits for which the project was created; to develop and use the deliverables specified for managing the project that are specified in the project management plan.

Project Team Meeting

What is it? A project team meeting allows everyone on the team to share goals and descriptions of upcoming work, report the status of his or her parts of the project, and to identify and resolve potential problems.

Purpose: To keep team members informed about the progress of the project; to have the team exchange updates on project progress; to resolve uncertainty that can cause delays; to propose and communicate pending scope, schedule, and cost changes that can affect team member assignments; to monitor the environment and anticipate problems; to review changes that are requested or required; to create a project status report for the sponsor, customer, and other stakeholders.

Monitor Project Progress

What is it? Monitoring is the process of keeping track of what is going on in and around the project to note issues, problems, trends, or incidents that could negatively—or positively—affect project progress. Monitoring is a management function and does not need to be carried out on a cyclical schedule; comparing the project's actual results against the plan is done at every level of the project: individual, subproject, and main project to meet project objectives.

Purpose: To proactively identify areas of the project's progress, management supervision, support, team performance, responsiveness, and quality that may need managerial involvement; to identify areas potentially requiring further investigation or action; to prioritize resources and attention to advance the project's progress; to apply corrective action immediately if appropriate; to adjust the system, support, or infrastructure of the project so it enables project success.

Progress Report

What is it? A project progress report captures information useful in managing and expediting the project objectives. These reports should be issued after the project team meeting and should reflect the consensus of the team on current progress. Stakeholders, particularly the customer and sponsor, need to be kept informed on the project's status, issues, and risks.

Purpose: To provide decision information; to keep the sponsor, customer, team members, and other stakeholders informed about the progress of the project; to document unresolved project issues. Normally, status reports are a recap of the results of the project team meeting. The status report shows the project "at a glance." You use it to confirm progress, note exceptions and variances, identify issues, and describe your planned action.

Meeting Evaluation Plan

What is it? Project teams need a way to capture suggestions from others in order to provide feedback to the leaders on how well the project is progressing. Meeting evaluation can also help team members run better meetings and meet the needs of the people doing the work. The meeting evaluation plan sets out the criteria or "ground rules" for effective meetings to ensure they support the work of the team and aid progress in meeting project goals. Methods of evaluation vary and can include forms completed at the end of a meeting by participants to online comments to verbal feedback on the agenda, depending on the group or the project work style.

Purpose: To determine how to guide the team, capture progress information, use information in decisions to continue project progress, and improve the project management process.

Project Status Report

What is it? The project status report is a periodic report based on the areas the project management plan must track. Status reports provide decision information from project team members and the project management scheduling system to highlight variances from the project plan and allow decisions on needed changes.

Purpose: To capture data in a consistent format and allow comparison between the progress that was expected and what is actually occurring, including the rate of expenditure of resources such as time and effort and expenses against what was allotted for creating the project deliverable(s).

Sponsor Review Meeting

What is it? Because the sponsor of the project is taking responsibility for the success of the project and the resources needed for its completion, sponsor review meetings are necessary to report the achievement of milestones within the project plan, the expenditure of resources against the budget, and any problems or issues that need sponsor involvement.

Purpose: To assure the project sponsor that objectives for the project are on target and progress is occurring as planned; or to address variations, issues that require sponsor involvement for resolution, changes in risk, as well as any key changes that might be needed to the project environment or the approved plan.

Customer/Sponsor Feedback

What is it? A project's success rests not only on completion of the deliverable of the project but also on the achievement of project goals and recognition of secondary benefits. Customer and sponsor feedback provides verification that these goals and benefits are on track. Methods may vary, to include survey questions, online responses, or verbal replies recorded by the team.

Purpose: To gauge whether the project team has completed its work, met the acceptance criteria for the final deliverables, and met the delivery dates and cost constraints, and may disband; to confirm that the deliverables and products of the project have been turned over to their owners; to confirm that the project sponsor has adequate information to determine goal achievement and conduct any necessary follow-up (for legal or regulatory requirements, and so forth, or for an ensuing project);

to confirm and/or refine the project process with customer and sponsor comments.

Project Closeout Report

What is it? The final project status report summarizes the project results: what was created and the disposition of the final project deliverables, the acceptance criteria met with any comments, the actual effort (hours) and cost (money) expended on the project, and the remaining resources, if any. It also confirms the deadline was met as projected in the schedule or identifies approved changes to that deadline with explanation.

Purpose: To document the project team's achievement of the project goals and objectives, as well as the use and disposition of the project deliverable products, and the deployment of the budgeted or assigned resources to allow project closure. It identifies the location of important information if follow-up should be needed, any improvements identified as needed in the project management processes, and the lessons learned for the benefit of future project teams.

APPENDIX  C

Projects vs. Operations

Projects differ from operations in several important ways. Operations—sometimes referred to as "doing business as usual"—is the normal way an organization conducts its daily business. Most organizations have a way to conduct business that was created specifically to do the work they are expected to do; however, while some are very repetitive, others—while repetitive—may allow customization to a specific situation or customer need. Let's look at some examples:

Production plant: Some organizations such as manufacturing plants have repetitive processes designed to perform a series of functions that create products or assemblies of products over and over again. Manufacturing plants design the process and align the equipment to do daily work with no customization and maximum efficiency. An example would be an automobile assembly plant.

Service business: Some organizations have operations that are repetitive but are capable of minor customization of products or services to suit a customer or group of customers. An example might be an insurance company producing insurance products customized to a particular customer's or company's insurance needs.

Custom products: Still, other organizations have operations that are repetitive in what they do but that nevertheless are capable of major customization of the product or service to suit a customer. An example might be a contract engineering firm, where products are designed for the customer organization; or an art-framing business, where the framing products and color and composition of materials are selected by the customer, but the framed art is assembled in a common way. Another might be a wedding caterer, providing select foods and desserts unique to a family's tastes and interests, yet which are prepared and delivered in a way common to weddings and customized to the specific type of wedding.

As a business develops its operations, many people develop a way to do the work, then improve the normal process incrementally over time, developing job descriptions of how the work that employees do is to be carried out. Documentation or automation of the processes the personnel follow is performed repetitively to generate the familiar products and services.

Projects, on the other hand, are often established to create something unique or different from what can be produced through normal operations. Because the work differs significantly from what has been done in the past, there may be no job descriptions for the work to be done. The project manager and team assemble a process and method of producing the end product, or "deliverable," using project management principles, then they manage the project using knowledge, skills, tools, and techniques defined by the project management profession, capturing lessons learned for use in the future.

A project that has never been done before provides very little structure to the people who perform the work on the project. Without experience doing similar work or creating similar outcomes, there is not much experience to draw from. The underlying process must be created as people discover how to do the work. Even if the project team records what they did, and records lessons learned after the fact, they do not benefit from that experience in advance.

A project may be created to do something that is unique but the team may be given a newly developed process to use in creating the structure for work. An example might be a project to develop a new product. There may already be a process for developing new products that can be adapted by the team with minor customization. Project management is applied to manage the unknowns, risks and variables inherent in developing that new product in its initial creation.

Some organizations have standardized the way they manage projects to reduce organizational risk. A project that is similar to other projects that have been carried out before may have a project management process template to guide the team. The steps in the process may be similar but what the team is creating may be unique, thereby requiring adaptations in the process to fit the new deliverable.

While there may be no defined job descriptions for the work to be done in creating the unique product or service on the project, there may be defined roles for the people on the team in organizations that do projects repeatedly.

For organizations that do different types of projects year after year, templates for the project management process may be available that can be customized for different types of projects. If the organization's project management maturity is high, the project team may be given job descriptions for the common types of jobs on the projects (e.g., project manager, project engineer, process engineer, scheduling specialist, or risk manager). There may even be project management process templates customized for the different types of projects the organization commonly does. As the process becomes more repetitive or familiar, efficiency increases.

In an automobile assembly plant, the equipment and jobs are sufficiently standardized that they can perform the same function over and over quickly and efficiently with very little risk or variation or process breakdown. Similarly, in an organization that performs projects regularly, the project management process carried out by the project manager and team can be captured in software and can be repeated from one project to the next. By customizing a template for managing each type of project—new product development, performing a development in a similar way but in a different location, and so on—the team becomes more efficient because at least some of the new functions in development have a familiarity to them and can be done more quickly.

The job description of the project manager and commonly used project management specialists allow these members of the team to perform the management of the project and other functions in a way similar to the roles they performed on prior projects, even though the product or service being created is different from what they had created before. This standardization helps team members work more efficiently. Although the project may be less efficient than what could be performed under normal operations, it is still more efficient than a team performing a project without a defined project management process.

Without an infrastructure, risk increases. As the infrastructure is standardized over time, the work carries less risk. Effective project management helps diminish this risk as much as the project team is capable of doing, but for organizations that value reducing project risk over time, putting an organization's project management infrastructure in place is a prudent path to follow. The most common way of improving the organization's overall infrastructure for projects is implementation of a Project Management Office or Program Management Office (PMO). There are a number of different models for a PMO. The establishment of such an office needs to be accomplished by creating a project for doing it; that way all of the requirements and expectations of management and the PMO's customers will be taken into consideration during the development process. After the PMO has been created and stabilized, it can be turned over to operations as another organizational staff function. For more information on the various structures of a PMO, and ways to advance organizational project management maturity, see *The McGraw-Hill 36-Hour Course: Project Management,* 2e © 2011 by Helen S. Cooke and Karen Tate.

About the Authors

Helen S. Cooke, MA, PMP, PMI Fellow

Independent consultant in management, project management, organizational project management maturity. Vice President Consulting Services, OPM Mentors—Chicago, IL. Instructor in Advanced Project Management at DePaul University and PM Systems at Keller Graduate School. Twenty years in project management, six years on PMI global board of directors, VP-Region II, headed PM delegation to South Africa. Past president of PMI Chicagoland Chapter and founder of Executive Council. Chair of Global PMI Council of chapter presidents, officer of PMI Educational Foundation. Developer/manager of *PMBOK Guide®* and *OPM3®*.

Helen was a manager for ten years at Deloitte, with three years each at McDonald's Corporation, American Management Systems, and United Airlines. She has 15 years in management consulting (corporate, government, high-tech, defense) and information systems project management. Throughout her management career, she has held various corporate positions in project management, including Program Manager, PMO Manager, Project Manager, Portfolio Manager, and Team Lead. She has provided management consulting to Fortune 500 companies such as Xerox Corporation and McDonald's Corporation; McDonnell Douglas Corporation; Pro Computer Sciences Corporation; the U.S. Army Command at Headquarters, Air Force Logistics Command; states of IL, KS, MN, MO, WI; and the Federal Deposit Insurance Corporation, U.S. Social Security Administration, and Department of Education of the U.S. Government. Prior to entering project management, she was a mid-level manager in the U.S. Federal government (Compliance Officer and Grants Manager), and a college administrator at Northwestern University. She was Finance Officer of the Chicago Phi Beta Kappa Association.

Helen served 10 years on both the *PM Journal* Editorial Board (PMI) and the board of the Project Management Institute's Educational Foundation. She was a PM keynote or speaker in New Delhi, Helsinki, Edinburgh, Rome, Capetown, Sydney, Denver, and Chicago.

Author of *The McGraw-Hill 36-Hour Course: Project Management,* 2e with Karen Tate, Helen has authored multiple technical articles and management handbooks, and was executive producer of two business films.

Karen Tate, MBA, PMP, PMI Fellow

Karen Tate, MBA, PMP, is the president and founder of The Griffin Tate Group, Inc. (TGTG), a WBENC-certified business (women-owned) and a Project Management Institute (PMI)® Charter Global Registered Education Provider (REP). TGTG specializes in training for the project management community using a practical, interactive approach to learning project management and leadership practices, processes, tools, and techniques to professionals at all levels, at companies around the world.

Prior to founding TGTG, she held various corporate positions in Project Management, Procurement, Construction, and Engineering. She has provided training and consulting with Fortune 500 companies such as General Electric, Bechtel Corporation, KFC corporation; DuPont, Procter & Gamble, Westinghouse, the Eli Lilly Company, Citigroup, and the Internal Revenue Service of the U.S. government.

Over the course of her career, Karen has helped thousands of students master the complexities of project management and the art of leadership. She is the coauthor of many highly regarded titles on the topic, including *Project Management Memory Jogger™; The Advanced Project Management Memory Jogger™; The McGraw-Hill 36-Hour Course on Project Management; Getting Started in Project Management; A Step-by-Step Approach to Risk Assessment;* and *Triz: An Approach to Systematic Innovation.*

Karen recently completed two consecutive terms of service on the PMI Global Board of Directors. In 2009, she received the PMI Fellow Award, PMI's highest and most prestigious honor, for sustained and significant contributions to PMI and the project management profession.